AT ARM'S LENGTH

Children's Literature Association Series

AT ARM'S LENGTH

A Rhetoric of Character in Children's and Young Adult Literature

MIKE CADDEN

University Press of Mississippi / Jackson

The University Press of Mississippi is the scholarly publishing agency of the Mississippi Institutions of Higher Learning: Alcorn State University, Delta State University, Jackson State University, Mississippi State University, Mississippi University for Women, Mississippi Valley State University, University of Mississippi, and University of Southern Mississippi.

www.upress.state.ms.us

The University Press of Mississippi is a member of the Association of University Presses.

Manufactured in the United States of America

First printing 2021
∞

Library of Congress Cataloging-in-Publication Data

Names: Cadden, Mike, 1964– author.
Title: At arm's length: a rhetoric of character in children's and young adult literature / Mike Cadden.
Other titles: Children's Literature Association series.
Description: Jackson: University Press of Mississippi, 2021. | Series: Children's Literature Association series | Includes bibliographical references and index.
Identifiers: LCCN 2021008826 (print) | LCCN 2021008827 (ebook) | ISBN 978-1-4968-3458-4 (hardback) | ISBN 978-1-4968-3459-1 (trade paperback) | ISBN 978-1-4968-3460-7 (epub) | ISBN 978-1-4968-3461-4 (epub) | ISBN 978-1-4968-3462-1 (pdf) | ISBN 978-1-4968-3463-8 (pdf)
Subjects: LCSH: Children's literature—History and criticism. | Persona (Literature) | LCGFT: Literary criticism.
Classification: LCC PN1009.A1 C26 2021 (print) | LCC PN1009.A1 (ebook) | DDC 809/.927083—dc23
LC record available at https://lccn.loc.gov/2021008826
LC ebook record available at https://lccn.loc.gov/2021008827

British Library Cataloging-in-Publication Data available

Contents

Acknowledgments

Nothing is really accomplished without help, and I'd like to acknowledge those who made the work not only easier but possible. So, here are those who share the blame for this:

Thanks go to my friends and colleagues Karen Coats, Kay Siebler, Roberta Seelinger Trites, and Dawn Terrick for reading and sharing notes and suggestions.

Thanks to my students in many sections of children's and young adult courses over the past several years. They not only helped me work through my arguments and examples but also offered other insights valuable to the development of ideas. They also often did that sideways head thing that dogs do when you are saying something new and weird to them.

Thanks to the folks at the Café Pony Espresso in St. Joseph, Missouri, the location for much of the writing, where I spent many wonderful Friday mornings writing and being left alone by the parts of the world that don't bring you food and coffee.

Thanks to the editors of *The Looking Glass: New Perspectives on Children's Literature* for allowing me to use portions of my essay from volume 17, number 2 and to the editors of *Children's Literature in Education: An International Quarterly* for allowing me to use portions of my article from volume 36, number 3 in this work.

This effort, along with so many others, is dedicated to the Brown-Eyed Ladies on Lovers Lane, St. Jo.

Preface

Often when we think of "literature for the young," we think of particular authors, such as Dr. Seuss, Maurice Sendak, or Beatrix Potter. Particular books spring to mind, such as *Goodnight Moon*, *The Snowy Day*, or *Tuck Everlasting*. Another association is with character. We often focus on the characters that populate our childhoods, like Pippi Longstocking, Matilda, or Arthur Read. In fact, we often distill a book or an author's entire works down to a single character. Rowling's series is simply known as "Harry Potter." Milne's books are known as "the Winnie-the-Pooh books."

This book attempts to understand the rhetorical appeal made to the reader through the modulation of arguably the most emotionally significant and affecting aspect of literature: character. What is the rhetorical effect of changing a character over the course of a book or an entire series of books, whether serial or episodic? When, why, or how does an author make a character more sympathetic, absurd, or larger than life? When less so? How is Junie B. Jones designed to appeal to us differently than Katniss Everdeen? Why does it matter? I want to consider children's characters as rhetorical gestures that are modulated (and sometimes not) by authors who want to, with the best of intentions, manipulate a young reader's sympathies. This book is an attempt to understand character change as a rhetorical modulation.

I first began to wonder about character effect on the reader when I was discussing Junie B. Jones with my university students. "She is so much like a first-grader!" they would argue. "That is so typical of little kids," they would say. This surprised me. I consider Junie to be a pretty exaggerated creature. I began to notice that students assumed young children would identify with Junie B. I, on the other hand, assumed young readers would laugh *at* her rather than *with* her. She's laughable, and you don't want to laugh at yourself, after all. At the same time, my students would argue that young readers *wouldn't* identify with Harry Potter because he was so extraordinary, but then why all the Harrys appearing at my door on October 31 for the last two decades? There was at work here some disconnect between adult assumptions about identification and what young people were doing with the texts. I started to notice and care about the differences between identification that was about projection (the desire to be or create a connection with a character) and identification that was recognition (actually seeing yourself in a character) and when there was to be no identification at all despite our enjoying the character immensely, such as our response to a Gargamel. It occurred to me that those three things were not only related but related in particular ways, and it's that observation that is the basis for this book.

It is my hope that the reader will regard this study as one of many useful tools available for considering character in young people's literature and culture; it is not my intention to suggest that this is *the* rhetoric of character in children's literature and culture but *a* rhetoric of character. It is my greater hope that readers will find applications for the ideas here that are only hinted at or not predicted at all. What I discuss may be important to the understanding of character in other literary contexts, so if it's useful in the study of a type of literature that I don't address, I am happy and grateful. What I say about character in this study might well apply to books for adults as well, but I'm discussing a phenomenon that I think is important in literature for the young.

My claims for character owe a great deal to Maria Nikolajeva's important book *The Rhetoric of Character in Children's Literature*, which stands as an implied antecedent to what I'm doing here. I think of that work as a taxonomy for the possibilities for character in children's literature. What I offer here is a consideration of how authors manipulate those characters in order to modulate the distances (measured by sympathy) between character and reader.

AT ARM'S LENGTH

Introduction

The Rhetorical Exchange

Literature for young people is characterized and regulated by distance—by holding children at arm's length or pulling them close. While the use of distancing effects is a phenomenon present in all literature, literature rhetorically situated because it's named for readers—"literature for young people" *relies* on textual and contextual distance in fundamental ways.

What do I mean by "distance"? First, we can acknowledge the more measurable textual distances: there is the type of narrative distance found between levels of story created by embedding or framing stories, and there are also the distances that exist between events and between characters, and those between story times and story spaces. We can also, as I do here, consider the rhetorical distance modulated between author and reader as well as the distance created and modulated between character and reader. By thinking and caring about "safe" and "appropriate" distances created in literature for the young (which we don't consider at all with literature for adults), we acknowledge the truly rhetorical nature of a genre named for readers. Naming a genre by its readership immediately calls to mind two ends of a rhetorical exchange. If this is *for* young people, then it's *from*, or offered up by, adults. Gifts have givers, after all. But there are those who would take away those gifts: censorship in the United States, for instance, is usually conducted in relation to children and their worlds—their classrooms, school libraries, and children's publishing houses—sites on par with the author regarding power and the relationship to the child. The "for" in "literature *for* young people" implies something about calculated distancing, and for that reason we shouldn't adhere to purely structural questions when discussing literature for the young. While literary critics who deal with literature generally might have misgivings about addressing authorial motivation, and have for the better part of the last fifty years, it is a major focus for people studying children's literature. Reports of the death of the author have been greatly exaggerated in children's literature.

The relationship between authors and young readers can be characterized by the nature of the pushmi-pullyu from *The Story of Dr. Dolittle*. The "pullyu" is at work when we hear and read the comments from our students, the media, and even our colleagues about how children's literature "draws in the reader," "pulls kids in," "makes kids identify," and—maybe the most ominous if the implications were considered—"makes a story come alive" (literally and dangerously in the cases of the books in the restricted section of the Hogwarts library or the characters in Cornelia Funke's *Inkheart*). When faced with the anthropomorphic in a children's book, adults will say that such characters draw in the young reader because, well, "kids love animals," "kids are like animals," or "kids can relate to animals" (or even that kids "*are* animals"). But there is also always a "pushmi." Maria Nikolajeva argues that for children to successfully understand what the author seems to want for them, "the balance of engagement and disengagement is a prerequisite" (*Reading for Learning* 89). Perry Nodelman also sees a tension that needs to be navigated in addressing the child reader that creates a balance between the "contradictory impulses" of being appeased and being challenged (*The Hidden Adult* 185). Reader, we want you to "fall into a book" and be "immersed," as the library posters tell you, but here's a bit of bungee, a life preserver, a narrative chain-link fence through which to look. The pushmi-pullyu is a creature drawn in two directions, after all, and balance is important for any creature, even those fantastical. So, in those larger arguments that critics have about how children's literature is or isn't different from other kinds of literature, I'd like to add to the list of defining features a consideration of this tension between drawing in and pushing away that happens in books for young readers. When we see one technique that seems intended to draw the reader in, we usually see an opposite (though not always equal) attempt to push away or hold back. So it might be fair to say that a "successful" book for young readers is one that balances the techniques of attraction and repulsion: it keeps readers within arm's reach but simultaneously at arm's length. With this notion of separation—a separation that is hierarchical—there is also an attendant agenda of protection. Invitation is accompanied by an uneasy knowledge that the invitation is sent to one who isn't the speaker/writer's equal—who isn't old enough to drive herself to the party and, once there, partake of all the refreshments.

An author might use different techniques to accomplish this balance of distances. For instance, in picture books like *Where the Wild Things Are* and *Arlene Sardine*, the author/illustrators provide a balance between potentially frightening language and subject matter with the comforting, cartoonish illustrations that mitigate that fear. Rosalyn Schanzer's award-winning nonfiction book on the Salem witch trials, *Witches!*, balances an engaging and questioning voice that involves readers in horrifying events with wood-cut illustrations that distance us through her use of folk-art symbolism. One quality of the book serves as pushmi (the pictures) to the pullyu of another (engaging language).[1]

The verse novel for young adults, a genre that has become a publishing phenomenon in the twenty-first century, offers an interesting site for examining this tension regarding distance. Techniques used to draw in the young adult (YA) reader include the inviting visual openness of the text, the sign-posting of section headers, lists of *dramatis personae* at the start (sometimes with convenient pictures of characters, as in the case of Karen Hesse's *Witness*), the use of enjambment and caesura to guide oral delivery and emphasis, a dialogue-driven narrative that is short on lengthy description, and the emphasis on character narration. The distancing techniques include the absence of description (which forces readers to rely on dialogue for all information), the tendency to rely on potentially confusing multiple character narrators, the fragmentation of presentation and action, the absence of plot sign-posting, and, well, the fact that at first glance it looks an awful lot like poetry. Because the genre in its contemporary incarnation is almost exclusively the province of literature for the young, we can question whether this is the case *because* of the balanced tensions of distance.

In some cases, however, the balance involves a single textual element. Above, I note how description's absence in the verse novel can be seen as both a draw and a barrier. Lars Bernaerts argues that the textual device of anthropomorphism offers a "*double dialectic* of empathy and defamiliarization" (69). Anthropomorphism is often used to both draw in readers and then also protect them. Gary Paulsen pushes us away at the opening of his autobiography *Woodsong* by showing us a wolf pack taking down a deer. He describes how he, upon witnessing this, was indignant at the "bad" wolves attacking the "innocent" deer, and he points out that we all tend to root for the deer and see the wolves as the villains, which Paulsen then goes on to argue is a misreading of the natural world that he lays on the doorstep of the anthropomorphic practices of children's literature (most notably Disney's). That said, later in his autobiography, he can't help but show his own sled dogs as clowns and dupes: one dog taunts another with a bone, consciously messing with another dog, and this would seem to draw the reader in by humanizing the dogs, which is what leads the author to give up eating meat—because animals are like *us*.

Anthropomorphism is one of the textual features that people use to define literature for the young, and yet there's little agreement about what it really does or what authors mean to do with it. Some argue that children relate to animals because they are vulnerable like themselves. Suzanne Keen argues that it isn't the animal to which readers connect, after all, but the humanized aspect of that animal (68). They connect *despite* the animal, which would argue that anthropomorphism is more a tool for distancing than for embracing. Lisa Rowe Fraustino has it that anthropomorphized characters act as screens or covers for messages and "allow humor and whimsy to disguise didactic messages" that point to "the child's own foibles" (148), which marks the technique as distancing. Lisa Sainsbury, in contrast, sees the animals in *Watership Down* used as a way to make issues of animal welfare more empathetic to young readers (128), which seems to be a technique of drawing in. I'll address the anthropomorphic in various places in my discussion of character in order to discuss its unique and vexing role in character–young reader distancing and in the rhetorical gestures of authors.

Another example of balance achieved through the use of one technique is found in the use of character narration, which can simultaneously draw in a young reader through the seduction of or identification with voice but even in the same text distance the reader from disturbing information by making the character narrator conveniently ignorant of some potentially disturbing details. Texts that easily come to mind that balance in this way include *Shiloh*, *The Borrowers*, and *The Hunger Games*. Character narration is typically reliable in literature for children, but the protagonist often simply doesn't know enough to stoke her own, much less the readers', fears about dire events. Child protagonists are simply not in a position to find out about or understand many adult actions. On the other hand, many would have it, my students included, that child narrators speak with a voice with which a child reader can identify and understand because "she's a kid like me."

A final example of a distancing technique is the use of intertextuality, which can be both distancing and inviting: the familiar text (one hopes) draws in a reader with recognition and familiarity and makes a great deal unnecessary to explain; however, there is also created a parallel that makes immersion in actual events difficult and protects the reader with metaphorical distance, as seen in the late Red Riding Hood chapter in Lois Lowry's *Number the Stars*. At the climactic moment in Lowry's Newbery-winning historical novel, the protagonist, Annemarie, must go through Nazi-infested woods to deliver an important package to her uncle. She uses the Red Riding Hood narrative to help create a distancing persona for herself (and the reader) while also using the comfort and attraction of the well-known narrative that the young reader will also know and love.

Annemarie doesn't make it clear whether she is referencing Perrault or the Grimms, though most children will know a version that ends happily rather than being gruesomely cautionary.

The author is the one responsible for creating and modulating the pushmi-pullyu of distance. As James Phelan observes, "there can be no rhetoric without a rhetor" (*Narrative Theory* 2); but the author has been unwelcomed or suspect in many literary circles since the New Critics—even if they have been quite welcome in personal appearances at meetings of the National Council of Teachers of English and Children's Bookstores Near You. Authority is something literary critics have been questioning most notably since Wimsatt and Beardsley decided that they were not amused with the Romantics and those people applying the work of Freud to the world of literature. Authority in children's literature is as contentious an issue as it is in all literature, but we can add to those usual objections the inequality of the relationship between adult writers and young readers as well as the rhetorical construction of the genre that complicates the question of whether one writes *for* or *to* or *at* or simply *near* children . . . or even acknowledges children at all. Managing distances between text and reader is how children's authors try to manipulate their younger, inexpert readers to have the relationships with stories that will keep them in the right balance of immersion and removal. It's a tricky balance to show the child reader a way toward power and yet keep from her the knowledge of her own powerlessness, to give her a glimpse of herself as vulnerable but one tempered by hope, to monitor the authorial power to enthrall but still provide a way out. I want to consider how some authors and critics address this notion of manipulation and then look at the ways that this rhetorical and textual manipulation happens through one story element: character.

Children's Writers' Notions of Authority

What gives a writer for children a sense of authority? Most writers for children are listened to as authorities regarding their own work and on the subject of writing for young people, although many writers for children echo their counterparts in the larger literary world by discounting any relationship they might have with the text once finished or with the reader at all. Many writers for children, however, see a relationship, *some* relationship, and hence an authority over the audience as well as with the text.[2]

The fear of didacticism, much maligned over the last century and a half as an authorial relationship to readers, is one reason authors often claim not to have any rhetorical agenda. Communicating with children is often equated with education rather than art. Claudia Mills points to two arguments against didacticism: children won't suffer it, and it doesn't work. "Moreover," she argues, "preachy presentations of goody-goody behavior may lead children to want to be naughty simply to distance themselves from unappealingly priggish protagonists. (Consider how much Tom Sawyer loathes Sid, the Model Boy of the village)" (2). Beverly Cleary herself observed that "as a child, [she] disliked books in which children learned to be 'better' children" (Stewart). Roger Collinson suggests that authority in children's literature is achieved through the writer's avoidance of the didactic, though he goes on to state that "the first essential of a book for children is that it must be a truthful book using language honestly" (38). Ursula K. Le Guin bemoans the fact that "the teaching impulse is often stronger than [she] is" ("A Response" 21). These criteria don't seem to be particular to children's literature, however; nor are these criteria very specific regarding how the author is granted authority through such "honest use of language." Wayne Booth opens *The Rhetoric of Fiction* with the caveat that he is "not primarily interested in didactic fiction, fiction used for propaganda or instruction" (xiii), which implies something disqualifying about the didactic as either rhetoric or literature. Addressing didacticism, however, is especially important to those who deal in children's literature.

One escape for the author from the "charge" of didacticism is for her to deny the aim of communication with children, and even the acknowledgment of audience entirely, claiming an allegiance to writers for adults who ostensibly don't have to worry about envisioning a readership. This is a sort of rhetorical bridge-burning and makes the case that the author can't discuss the audience in ways that might be of interest or of use to him or her, such as acknowledging actual communication from young readers in the forms of fan letters, reports from teachers or parents, or input from editors and publishers about what has been successful with or appreciated by child readers in the past—readers different enough from the writer to warrant the author's desire for more information about them. Maurice Sendak famously denied writing for children—or any external audience—as he did in his interview with Stephen Colbert: "I don't write for children. I write. And someone says, 'That's for children'" (Colbert). H. A. Rey claims *himself* as audience: "I know what I liked as a child, and I don't do any book that I, as a child, wouldn't have liked" (Houghton Mifflin). Nina Bawden makes the case for the technique of focalization as the determination of whether she writes "for children" by saying that the "only real difference between writing for adults or for children is whose eyes I am looking through" (191). Ursula K. Le Guin also points to focalization when she says that she had to see the story of Earthsea through the character of Therru: "Until I saw Therru, until she chose me, there was no book. I couldn't see the story till I could look through her eye" (*Earthsea Revisioned* 19). Jill Patton Walsh believes that while the author is "primary" in an implied literary hierarchy of writer, text, and reader ("The Writers in the Writer" 4), the author divides her authority with the narrator, who "obliterates the flesh-and-blood author" (6). Walsh claims that "on finishing the book, the author lays aside the narrator's mask, and has henceforth no special claim upon the book, no special relationship with it other than a remembered one" (8).[3]

So, some authors communicate with nobody; some communicate with their past, younger selves; others make the case that it is technique that makes the difference, which is defined by others; others communicate with their art. These authors are merely conduits for stories to come into the world. They report what the muses tell them. They stumble upon characters over whom they have no control rather than allow them voice. They are Michelangelo, chiseling characters out of text. They are enthralled, literally, and simply must follow where they are led. They don't communicate with readers named by the genre in which they write. When I consider these positions in the context of "children's literature" in particular, I find them terribly disingenuous. It might be one thing to claim that in the initial hot flash of creativity that audience isn't a consideration, but in the cool and sober awareness of revision of a piece identified by an agent or editor as "for young readers," it seems unlikely if not irresponsible that the implications for the reader remain unconsidered. In a short article entitled "Intention," Philip Pullman argues that authorial intention is a difficult business to settle. He doesn't consider intention a function of communication, most specifically communication to young. It's worth noting that his article was solicited for a book about children's literature. He seems willing to acknowledge responsibility, though for a broader audience: "To disclaim intention and responsibility altogether seems to me to regard the author as little more than an elaborate piece of voice-recognition software, taking down dictation form an unseen source. Of course our intentions matter to some extent: it's just rather difficult to say what they are" (132). This unease with the extent to which intention matters is likely a function of an unease about, or an unwillingness to name, an audience, perhaps for fear of limiting it. He asks whether "age-guidance of any sort [implies] that the book is intended for a particular kind of reader" and decides that "hope" rather than "intent" is the right word to use here. In other words, the author is casting out into the void with the hope that the right fish will find the lure but then this suggests that the same bait works for all fish and that a good fisherman might not know the difference between a body of water in which you find trout and one in which you find marlin (132). Hemingway's Santiago not only knew what fish he was after, but he spoke directly to it the whole time. He knew his audience, he named it, and he respected it.

Other authors find less difficulty in linking responsibility to intent because they acknowledge a clearer sense of audience. Terry Pratchett, a crossover writer by genre and audience, keeps it rather murky: "There's a lot difference between writing for children and writing for adults, and it's almost impossible to tell you what it is, but I know it when I'm doing it. You have more fun, and I have to say, it's a little bit harder, especially if you do it right" ("Talking with Terry Pratchett," *A Hat Full of Sky* 228). As we see with Pratchett, some authors for children who *do* acknowledge a difference often claim that writing for children is *more* difficult than writing for adults or that children are a tougher audience. Mark Haddon has it that "writing for children is bloody difficult; books for children are as complex as their adult counterparts, and they should therefore be accorded the same respect." Madeleine L'Engle claimed that the book has to be written the way it "wants to," but then adds that "if the book will be too difficult for adults to swallow, then I will write it in a book for children" (*A Circle of Quiet* 198) which challenges the Walsh-like claims about the book doing what it wants and the author's control over her audience. While some authors may be protesting too much against a perceived notion that it is easier to write for children, at least these claims suggest that they take the act of artistic communication seriously.

James Phelan and Peter Rabinowitz take issue with this "mythology that serious artists don't pay attention to their audiences but instead focus only on expressing their visions." They go on to protest that "it's impossible to make meaningful rhetorical choices without some sense of whom you are addressing" (139). In this context of a rhetorical view of literature, Richard Walsh argues that "the abdication of creative control is also a release from moral accountability" (133), which is convenient for those unwilling to assume that accountability. Authors like Katherine Paterson, Ursula K. Le Guin, Roger Collinson, and Mollie Hunter believe that the writer has a special, moral responsibility to the child readers; the writer must avoid the act of didacticism discussed above. In many cases, the distinction between ethical fiction for children and didacticism lies in a sort of self-imposed ethical or "moral boundary" the author recognizes regarding what can and ought to be handled, and how.[4] In these writers' cases, however, protection is accomplished by careful stylistic treatment of life's difficulties rather than by the thematic elision of censorship or the stylistic condescension of preaching. Such writers attempt morally responsible yet intellectually provocative art for children, aims these authors find neither paradoxical nor mutually exclusive. Le Guin, Paterson, and Hunter all buy into Roger Collinson's observation that because "the writer of children's books . . . cannot ignore his readers" (42), that writer owes it to the child to be his "brother's keeper" (43).

This "keeping," or protection, is manifested in the "special care" (Hunter 18) the writer takes in not subjecting the child reader to the particular psychoses, phobias, or problems the author herself hasn't yet worked through, which is that pushing away or distancing at work. Many children's writers see the dialogic responsibility of the writer for the child audience to be closer to a communications model of literature rather than a purely romantic and aesthetic model. Roger Collinson says much the same thing when he asserts that "it is surely indefensible for an author to work out his own *adult* problems and hangups in a book for children. This would be unacceptable self-indulgence" (43), which highlights the fact that the artist in this scenario is a communicator and not someone who is "working through" something in print for an unacknowledged reader. The author for children whose authority derives from her sense of responsibility is antecedent to the text and is for the purpose of communicating with the reader, potentially beginning a dialogue.

Katherine Paterson is adamant in her take on the same issue and on the distinction between the didactic and the moral: "I will not write a book that closes in despair. I cannot, will not, withhold from my young readers the harsh realities of human hunger and suffering and loss, but neither will I neglect to plant that stubborn seed of hope" (38). She works in the tradition of Dickens and James, who Martha Nussbaum notes "closely connect the stance of the author to the stance of the reader—as the authorial presence occupies in thought and feeling the reader's position, asking what the reader will be able to feel and think" (8). Authors for children employ empathy for the audience as they create characters that inspire empathy from the reader. Hope, these writers would argue, is not a violation of realism. The literary myopic is the author who dismisses the reader that designates the genre in which she operates. Mollie Hunter reflects this with the observation that writing to children is "freedom with responsibility" (23)—a responsibility other kinds of authors don't see. Because these writers for children define their literary and specific generic task in terms of their genre's audience designation (rather than in terms of a general aesthetic of literature), they find that their authority is fueled by, but also answerable to, an audience.

While some authors for children eschew moral responsibility by denying a rhetorical relationship with the reader, others embrace both the rhetorical and ethical responsibility while claiming that this can be done without didacticism. Is creating distance a matter of didacticism or protection? While a writer might claim not to be trying to teach the reader, mightn't she make matters more accessible to the reader by modulating the distance between content and reader? In other words, rhetorically minded authors can still monitor how close readers get to things. Suzanne Keen posits that "fictional worlds provide safe zones for readers' feeling empathy without experiencing a resultant demand on real world action" (35) and that it might require "repeated entrances into fictional worlds" in order to benefit young and developing readers (72). Authors create safe zones through distancing in order for young readers to process ideas without trauma or the need to act in any particular way. It isn't preaching as much as guidance. The ethics involved in this is clear; in fact, Maria Nikolajeva goes so far as to suggest that "all children's fiction is ethical," and in this regard the greatest problem is for us to understand the implied reader (*Reading for Learning* 179, 195).[5]

A Rhetorical Approach

For all of the reasons addressed above, genres named for readers require authors to consider their authority, what it means to communicate with readers different from themselves by age, and the ethical responsibility to do this well, however that might be defined. Children's literature has no less than other literary contexts been subject to post-Romantic era calls for ignoring authors. Children's literature scholarship and criticism have come of age in eras of structuralism and poststructuralism. It has been divided between book and child people, and we have professional academic divisions separating those working in departments of English, library science, and education—people who have sometimes defined their work and professional lives by being either book or child advocates, respectively. To work in children's literature in English has often meant adhering to a rhetoric-free mission and leaving affective theories to people who work with children. So, added to those authors who claim to write to nobody we have had academic traditions from New Criticism to postmodernism that have been all too happy to oblige in erasing the communications exchange. Wayne Booth pointed to this problem: "This act of communication, fundamental to the very existence of literature, has in modern criticism often been ignored, lamented, or denied. True artists, we have been told again and again, take no thought of their readers" (*The Rhetoric of Fiction* 89).

To consider a rhetorical approach to children's literature is not to say that structure is unimportant; in fact, a rhetorical approach acknowledges that structure is a means to an end, and one end is persuading children to think or see or feel things, whether that is achieved or not. Seymour Chatman contrasts the rhetorical and the merely structural in this way:

> In attaching "rhetoric" to *technique*, however, we must not imply that the rhetoric of fiction deals with different materials than its grammar. The materials are the same: rather, rhetoric looks at those materials from a different perspective. It is not concerned so much with the definitions of techniques like narrative voice or flashback but with the showing how they apply to the text's end—the set of explicit and implicit suasions of the implied reader. (44)

James Phelan distinguishes the structuralist and the rhetorician by saying that the former seeks an objective view of the text, "one which foregrounds the text as a construct, the mimetic analyst takes a rhetorical view, one which foregrounds the text as communication between author and reader" (*Reading People, Reading Plots* 8). To consider only structure is to pay attention only to the audience implied by the existing structures of a work. A rhetorical consideration takes into account "the presuppositions and beliefs that operate for the different audiences that are always present" (Phelan, *Reading People, Reading Plots* 140–41), and the young audience is not merely a structural marker of genre or a coincidental implication but a reminder to anyone working in its environs that there is a real, young person reading this work, a person fundamentally different from the author in age, experience, maturity, and cognitive development. James Phelan explains that a rhetorical approach to narrative "assumes that texts are designed by authors in order to affect readers in particular ways" (*Experiencing Fiction* 4). He also distinguishes between rhetorical device and outcome: "The phrase 'narrative as rhetoric' means something more than that narrative uses rhetoric or has a rhetorical dimension. It means instead that narrative is not just story but also action, the telling of a story by someone to someone on some occasion for some purpose" (*Narrative as Rhetoric* 7). The children's author's purpose will be varied, to be sure, but it's clear that whatever is communicated is going to be modified based on the very fact that the audience is comprised of young people. Once hearing the command, "Don't think of elephants," one must; it seems fair to suggest that "children's literature" functions in the same way for authors; children are the elephants in the room of children's literature. The authorial audience for children's writers is guaranteed to be children, regardless of what other audiences are implied or simply occur (and there surely are multiple audiences intersecting the one age-based). There is, as a rhetorical context, a kind of recursive relationship that is modulated by both parties—which might be over the course of a book, a series, or a children's author's collected works.[6] James Phelan uses the term "progression" to describe narrative as a "dynamic event" that "must move, in both its telling and its reception, through time" (*Reading People, Reading Plots* 15). There will be "instabilities" between characters in story and "tensions" in discourse and between author, narrator, authorial audience that will show how the author is modulating distance between the young audience and the text.

A rhetorical approach has to start with a structural acknowledgment of the implied reader and author but push past the structural to the contextual, to the authorial audience. Peter Rabinowitz explains authorial audience in this way: "The notion of the authorial audience is clearly tied to authorial intention, but it gets around some of the problems that have traditionally hampered the discussion of intention by treating it as a matter of social convention rather than of individual psychology" (*Before Reading* 22). The genres of literature for young people are founded on social convention necessarily. Richard Walsh argues that a "rhetorical perspective implies a concern with communicative acts, which in Booth's terms meant the 'glorious meeting' of authors and readers in texts" (403). He notes that this glorious meeting, so easily envisioned in the literary context of literature for young people, is to be understood in terms of context rather than simply intention. A literary act should be "marked by the specificity of its occasion," and in this way, the "authorial role is somewhat refigured (5). For him, and for me, the authorial response to a literary occasion—in this case "writing for young people"—must be acknowledged. Barbara Wall would have it that "the real author knows only the implied reader, a presence his or her text inescapably calls into being; the real reader knows only the implied author, whose all-embracing presence pervades the book he or she reads" (7), and this is in keeping with Jill Paton Walsh's complaint that she can't know the reader. So while Wall is not wrong to claim that "the narrator-narratee relationship, rather than that of implied author and implied reader, is the distinctive marker of a children's book" (9), it is incomplete without saying that authorial modulation of story—especially of character—is a distinctive marker of writing for children. There are, in other words, distinct markers or structures as well as distinct acts and balances within and through the creation of those structures.

What follows is a description of a particular rhetoric of character for literature for the young that rests on the claims made here about the rhetorical exchange between adult and child, the authority and ethical responsibility adult authors claim in that relationship, and what it means to pursue a rhetorical approach in this literary context.

1

A Rhetoric of Character

There are obviously a great many literary elements and techniques that can be viewed rhetorically. Narrative point of view and plotting are useful contexts for considering the ways children's writers communicate and manipulate distance between child reader and text, for instance, but I would like to consider characterization as a particularly important and useful communication technique in children's literature. I would go so far as to say that as character goes, so goes the rhetorical relationship between author and reader. Mieke Bal argues that "character is intuitively the most crucial category of narrative, and also most subject to projection and fallacies" (115). Robert Scholes has it that "to suggest that one order of characterization is better than another is folly. To recognize that differences exist is the beginning of wisdom" (161); I hope to show more wisdom than folly.

As teachers, scholars, and readers, we need to be clear that realism as a setting (the usual definition of "realism") doesn't mean that all characters are to be regarded as representational by default.[1] This may seem like an obvious point, but it might well be news to writers of some children's literature handbooks, who often imply, if not state outright, that character in children's realism is automatically assumed to require or foster identification from the reader (and a bad form of it at that) *because* characters are assumed to be mimetic simply by being in text with a realistic setting. E. M. Forster counters that "[characters] are real not because they are like ourselves (though they may be like us) but because they are convincing" (62), and they can be convincing in a number of ways that have nothing to do with being like us or people we know. To be "convinced" might mean that we accept their function as well as (or in spite of) the degree to which they have dimension, and that function isn't necessarily to be an object of identification.

When educators and publishers discuss diversity, there is sometimes the simple goal of having children "see themselves" represented in fiction, but different readers can be drawn in and pushed away for an array of reasons that go beyond the demographic similarity of characters. As I discussed earlier, the phenomenon of drawing in and pushing away for different readers can happen simultaneously, surely, but later I'll say more about the risks of assuming something is being communicated simply through the choice of character demographics.[2]

As children's books have become more about identification than sources for role models, identification has become a value in assessing children's books' success by teachers, parents, and publishers. "A child can relate" has become higher critical praise than "This character provides a good role model for readers." Suzanne Keen has argued that "novels that succeed in invoking strong character identification are likelier to reach large numbers of readers" and that "Middlebrow readers tend to value novels offering opportunities for strong character identification" (11). *Children's Literature, Briefly*, by Tunnell and Jacobs, asserts that "of all the genres in children's literature, contemporary realistic fiction is the most popular [because] people are interested in their own lives, and this genre is about 'my life. This is my world. This is how I live. This story is about a girl like me'" (128). They go on to claim that "the importance of identifying with one's own life is a reason children's books have children as protagonists" (129).[3] Identification becomes associated not only with critical success but with the genre of realism as well, and this has helped make realism the more "literary" or serious genre. Genre is simply not a good measure for whether a character will invite closeness or distance to a reader. Any genre can create characters that draw us close or push us back.[4] James Phelan reminds us of something that should be obvious: characters are constructs, and we should not limit their success at inspiring identification to certain genres (Phelan, *Reading People, Reading Plots* 3).

There are, as alluded to above, quantitative and qualitative forms of representational character. Quantifiable forms of representation are often what could be called surface or visible descriptions, though that doesn't at all make them unimportant. They tend to be demographic. The most important demographic in children's literature is the child.[5] Following that, other quantifiable elements include race, gender, ethnicity, religion, regional affiliation/location, culture, and other markers that have tangible, visible qualities that contribute to character dimension and description. When people call for diversity in children's books, this is often what is focused on, and unfortunately often the only thing. Quantifiable representation obviously varies in the degree to which it is described and made important in the text. Franklin in the Peanuts series is quantifiably darker skinned than the other characters, but that is as far as his difference through representation goes. At its worst, quantifiable representation is used to check boxes; at its best it is a means for enabling child readers to recognize differences and the fullness of the world. Qualitative representation, in contrast, is less visible and deals with more subjective qualities, such as a character's reported history or experience, personality, interests, and thoughts. While being an orphan would be fairly quantifiable, being lonely and misunderstood by family would be a bit more subjective and less "visible," for instance. Being bookish (a popular form of representation for readers of books, after all), "dorky," resilient, and loyal are identifiable qualities, but these qualities are not as easily quantified or seen immediately (granted, the presence of glasses on a character or a book in her hand is often a symbolic quantification meaning "nerd"). Quantifiable representations are more easily noted by potential purchasers or browsers looking through illustrations; qualitative features may need to be commented on in book blurbs or through recommendations and book reviews to be communicated to potential readers. You can't know that you'll identify with a character's shyness from looking at the cover.

One form of representation, either the quantitative or qualitative, will almost always play a role in how the other develops. Being "different" can be quantified in a character, but it might lead to the significant qualitative marker of loneliness or "being misunderstood" that a reader might identify with even if the quantitative representation doesn't match up with the reader; so, too, the reader might "see herself" in the quantitative representation of "being short" but finds nothing else in that character to connect to, perhaps because the character is brutish and nasty as well as short. The belief that simple, quantifiable representation is sufficient to connect with readers is as problematic as the assumption that realistic settings and circumstances necessitate that characterization will be realistic. In fact, in some cases, readers will simply disregard quantitative representation made clear by the texts. Two infamous examples of misreadings of the quantifiable include dark-skinned characters. Ursula K. Le Guin's wizard Ged is described as "copper-brown" (19) in *A Wizard of Earthsea* but is often visually depicted in film and book covers as the generic white-skinned wizard. The dark-skinned character Rue in *The Hunger Games*, who was also depicted as dark skinned in the film version, was the subject of complaints by moviegoers who glossed the description of her on page 40 and inserted their own racial image of "cute, little girl" (aka, white). So when skin color is a brief description but not part of the qualitative characterization in the book—when it's made (or perceived to be) incidental to character—it can not only be missed but actually overwritten by folks who create their own quantifiable objects of either preference or identification.

An author can use quantitative and qualitative characterization as a means to modulate the distance between the text and the reader. The author can communicate by offering up characterization that is meant to provide quantifiable distance (difference) or perhaps closeness (sameness). The author can also communicate that through qualitative descriptions that will invite sympathy or indifference. The author can rely on combinations of these things as well: a character quantifiably different from majority culture (which, in fantasy, might mean being an elf or troll) might have highly sympathetic or identifiable desires or qualities, for instance, like being afraid of the dark.

It's important to recognize that it isn't always (or maybe even usually) the most representational of characters that inspire emotional responses. Despite the author's use of distance to create an identification barrier between text and reader, we often have the phenomenon of bathos at work. The most powerful version is found in fake or superficial realism. In recent years in the United States we have seen the development of a genre of video that could be called "military parent appears in a school." The scene requires little to trigger an emotional response from a war-weary population appreciative of its soldiers and concerned for their children. A child is identified in a gym, a ball field, or a classroom, and then a uniformed (important detail) adult appears in a doorway or out of a crowd. The child recognizes the uniformed adult and runs to him or her. The scene climaxes with hugs and tears. The viewer experiences sudden allergies (red eyes, tears, sniffles). While there is nothing cheap, insincere, or wrong with the larger context of this scene (for the actual student and soldier, it is powerful stuff, of course), it merely works as symbols of emotion for the reader. Bathos, as a literary device, is a cheap trick, so to speak, to make us cry at undeveloped but highly symbolic representations. Any number of examples exist in generic form, though usually "realistic" and involving the vulnerable: a child dying of cancer; a deathbed forgiveness; an innocent child lead astray; a sacrificial death for a cause dear to the reader.

In my discussion below, I'll be distinguishing between unreal characters that may, however, involve highly qualitative character representation (Hobbits that you come to love for their developed and individual natures) as well as characters set in realism who are quantitatively exaggerated, loveable, but not the objects of identification. In other words, within a system of characterization that charts spatial relationships between the real, unreal, and exaggerated in character, it is important to note how they work as distancing tools used by authors to modulate the distance between text and reader.

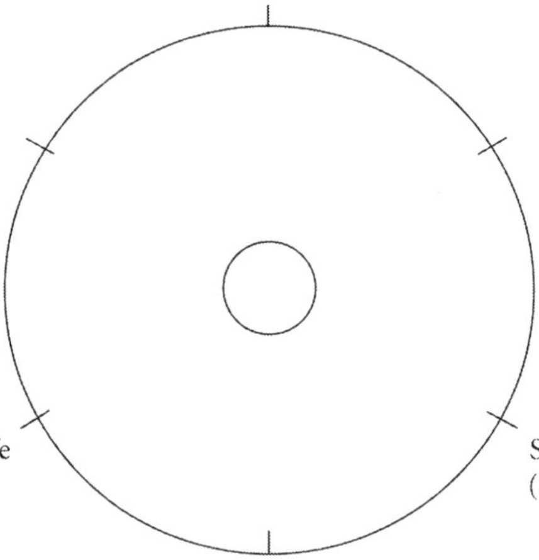

Diagram 1

My focus in this project is on the rhetorical function of character for the authorial audience of children's books rather than as rhetorical agents themselves within their stories. What do authorial choices regarding characterization, in particular, mean for how the reader is to position herself relative to the story? What can we make of a character's change of function over the course of a story for young people or even over the course of a series as opposed to the questionable claims that characters "grow," for instance? I want to propose a figure that represents something of a "dialing up" of character construction—a way to think about how an author writing to a young audience might modulate and manipulate character in any genre to move readers inward through empathy or distance them through either the funhouse mirror of exaggeration or larger-than-life unreality.

Diagram 1 offers a way to think of movement and modulation of character as rhetorical. The modulation of character over narrative and real time, as well as the positioning of characters in relation to others, is made in order to have an effect on the audience. The diagram represents how characters can be manipulated or modulated to balance indifference, pity, sympathy, and empathy in order to create the desired distance between reader and text, and it will do that by manipulating both quantitative as well as qualitative representation.

Let's begin at the apex of "the dial," so to speak. If realistic, lifelike characters are now to be considered measurable by reader identification, let's say that the representational character is designed by the author to communicate to the reader the most opportunity for sympathy, or even empathy. So, it might be that the author wants the reader to come "closer" to character by creating one that is round, psychologically rich, developed in dimensions including idiosyncrasies and descriptions of behavior and appearance, and adds to that over the course of a story or series of stories. These characters are possible, probable, plausible, and aren't modulated toward exaggerated or superhuman behavior, abilities, morality, or intelligence. They may be quantifiably representative in a number of ways, including race and gender that marks an attempt by the author either to draw in through identification or just not push away by making the character too unlikely or unusual. Sometimes, however, an author modulates ("turns the dial") from the lifelike toward smaller than life or the larger than life by degree if they wish to make characters more memorable but less likely, and less sympathetic. Importantly, any rhetorical goals an author has regarding multiculturalism will be affected by dialing in one direction or another either in terms of physical depiction or quality of behavior. Characters can be made larger than life or smaller to achieve different rhetorical ends.

• • •

If we turn the dial from representationalism or "life sized" to the larger than life, we see a different effect and message to the reader. This modulation creates the character that is the prodigy, the genius, the spy kid, the one gifted beyond our comprehension. Here we have Encyclopedia Brown or secret agent Alex Rider in Anthony Horowitz's popular *Stormbreaker* series. These are not characters exaggerated from some aspect of human behavior as much as simply unreal in their possession of abilities that aren't available to children or even to most adults. Maria Nikolajeva asserts that such characters—"high mimetic" in Northrop Frye's terms—"are supposed to serve as models not only for the other characters in the story but for the readers as well" (*Rhetoric* 33), and, of course, modeling doesn't require empathy. In fantasy, these characters tend to be demigods, superheroes, wizards, or something new on the earth, like Charles Wallace in *A Wrinkle in Time*, Will Stanton in *The Dark Is Rising*, or Ender Wiggin in *Ender's Game*. Stereotype isn't as likely a concern here. They can be Good or Evil. Here, as with extreme exaggeration, our response is likely a broad choice between approbation and disdain, not recognition of ourselves. The extreme characters of exaggeration or superhumanity are not recognizable as us, and the closer to that position the character goes, the more clearly the author is communicating this to the child reader.

This all said, a consistently surprising response is offered up by both children and college students to these exaggerated and unreal characters in realism. If identification can be a *projection* as much as it can be *recognition*, and sympathy or empathy can follow projection, as Suzanne Keen explains in *Empathy and the Novel*, then there is some explanation for what some adults do with the exaggerated character and what some children do with the unreal, larger-than-life character. Keen wonders "whether mature readers feel differently about fictional characters as they grow up, or whether they learn to assess and present their responses differently" (111). I think they do both of these things, and in relation to children. In my experience discussing books with both children and adults, I have found that the adults are the ones most likely to mistake the extremely exaggerated child character as typical and representational: "Oh, that Junie B. Jones is just like the six-year-olds in my class. They are all *so funny*." The adult accepts this exaggerated portrayal (which could stereotype children) and then projects identification on behalf of the child reader, which enables those adults to say that children can and will "relate" to Junie, which is, as handbooks reinforce, almost always also a claim of approval for children's realism. Children, on the other hand, don't typically claim Junie B. as "like them," much less "good" for that reason, but simply note that she is silly and funny—a laughable and ridiculous creature. Children can approve of and like Junie while they laugh at her, but I don't think they necessarily empathize with her. As fable morals are really for those other people who need them, exaggerated characters are not us.

The larger-than-life character in children's fiction is, in contrast to the smaller-than-life character, not likely to inspire adults to project identification on behalf of a child reader. My adult students (many of whom are nontraditional by age) don't assume that Alex Rider, boy secret agent, or the legendary Maniac Magee are going to be "relatable" to children. The unreal character will be deemed either implausible or accepted as the character *necessarily* implausible for the story. The child reader, however, may well be unsure of the actual implausibility or even impossibility of such a character and, in seeing its portrayal in a realistic setting and, well, its extreme coolness, *project* identification through desire and wish fulfillment and build empathy. A child reader is likely to play Alex Rider, not pretend to be Junie B. Jones. Halloween costumes, the ultimate wish-fulfillment-projected identification, are more likely to depict larger-than-life rather than exaggerated characters, and by wearing the costume, the child indicates her desire to inhabit that character. So, there is across two readerships a double dialectic in response to character distance.

Consider Marc Brown's popular "Arthur" books. In this case, we see the main character begin literary existence closer to the "unreal" category given his anthropomorphism (he is an aardvark) though real in his attending human school. It is the realistic setting and context that creates the pull, the drawing in; it is the use of both cartoon and anthropomorphism that provides the push, the holding at arm's length. As the years roll on, Marc Brown alters his rhetorical relationship with his perceived reader and slowly removes the anthropomorphism in the text by degree, making Arthur more and more representational a figure. His problems are no longer aardvark related, like having his long nose get in the way as it does in the first book. It's almost as if Brown finds less and less need for keeping the reader at arm's length, as though he tested a rhetorical relationship and has modulated it over time. He can't convert Arthur into a real boy in Pinocchio fashion, but Arthur has gone from being an actual aardvark to a kid with weird ears who shares Voldemort's rhinoplasty specialist. No new reader exposed to a recent Arthur book would ever guess his species.

Speaking of his lordship, he is another example of a character that over narrative and publication time travels from unreal toward representational (but never gets there). Voldemort begins as a rather unreal entity. He begins to move from abhorrent, unreal villain to a fellow who had a more realistic (and sympathetic) response to childhood abuse than even Harry did. Of course, we neither want to be Voldemort nor see ourselves in him, but Rowling slides him along the scale toward the life sized ever so slightly, so that the reader is drawn closer to him through an awakening pity. Rowling apparently wants him to mean something different later in the series, and she creates for us a different connection with him. It is important to note that she does this late in the series through the literary device of back story: Voldemort's childhood is long past and only revealed (created) when she wants his character to change in order to create an emotional closeness she must now deem useful and safe. She could have dialed him from the larger than life in the direction of smaller rather than life sized, making him a comic villain and absurd and sad like that Gargamel fellow chasing smurfs, but that communicates something entirely different to us; arguably, she does do this at the very end of the series. This is about changing a message and a readerly relationship. Voldemort doesn't grow; he changes function thematically and mimetically, and Rowling modulated that character message. In fact, she seems bent on continuing to do that postpublication. Are we only *now* ready for a gay Dumbledore and a Jewish Hogwarts professor? I'll say more about backstory in chapter 2.

It's not just between the larger than life to life sized that characters move, of course. However, I do think children's writers show an inclination, especially over the course of a book series, to move toward sympathetic reality from either the direction of the smaller or larger than life as authors decide that they want to draw in readers emotionally rather than maintaining a safe distance—almost as if there is a test period that they wait out to find out how real they can get and for what purposes. It's what we see in long-running sitcoms, for instance (*M*A*S*H*, *Roseanne*, *Friends*). People get less exaggerated and more real over narrative time, like Joey Pigza and Anne Shirley. They don't grow; their functions change as the authors want to communicate something different. Perhaps only over time do some authors become ambitious about message and seriousness.

The character occupying a space between the larger than life and the smaller than life has no direct route toward the lifelike—you can't get there from here—and that also has rhetorical purpose and effect. Such a character—that Gargamel alluded to above, or the Master in the Doctor Who series—is at once both the most removed and distant character from the reader rhetorically and empathetically. That such laughability and awesomeness combined is so common in texts *for* children may indicate that safety is a high value in children's media. The character ensconced between smallness and largeness is the sort we can present on television to the child while we make dinner. It's safe because it is the least connected to reality.

In the chapters that come, I'll be examining the modulations made by authors in their rhetorical relationship with the authorial audience. My goal is not to create a strictly taxonomical system for defining children's literature, which Marah Gubar has shown to be a particular idiosyncratic folly of our discipline ("On Not Defining"), but to show under a particular framework that we can see the rhetorical shifts made by authors of children's texts. What does it mean for characters to become more qualitatively representative over the course of a book or series? What accounts for the popular character of the "silly madman" or funny mad scientist in texts for children? Why is there disagreement on the identification potential of exaggerated characters set in realism? Because I'll be talking about differences of degree more than kind, a set of firm rules for what all texts mean seems less useful than describing a tool for considering individual texts across age and genre, though it can be useful to identify a "type" of character as well, if even by degree.

Chapter 2 begins with an examination of the lifelike and examines the movement between sympathy and the larger than life. What is achieved by constructing and modulating character along this curve? If we acknowledge that characters do not "grow" or "mature" as much as authors modulate their function, what does it mean for characters to become more or less representative or decidedly unrepresentative as characters? What might inspire the modulation of character from "real" to "unreal" or the reverse? Does it matter in what genre the case exists? The use of anthropomorphism is especially interesting in this category as there are different degrees of quantitative representation offered in children's books, and the degree to which we have "people in fur" like Arthur Read or animals in a human world but in possession of human consciousness like Black Beauty come into play here. Anthropomorphism is examined here as a distancing technique particular to the rhetorical modulation of "real" and "unreal" for children. Anthropomorphism in one fashion or another is addressed in each chapter as it is a phenomenon of character in children's literature that exists across all character formations.

Chapter 3 examines the relationship by degree between the lifelike and the ridiculous and smaller than life. It is here that the choices authors make about extreme traits will be examined. What does it mean to make a character more or less ridiculous (in contrast to the potential seriousness that the larger than life carries with it)? What is communicated to readers regarding their own and others' natures? Here, especially, questions of stereotype and diversity are discussed. What are the implications for representation of diversity to and for different audiences when exaggeration is in play?

Chapter 4 plays with the no man's land regarding representation. The character that makes the turn, so to speak, coming from either the ridiculous or larger than life to the space between is a character devised to be the most distant from representation. What does this distance serve in children's fiction? What is communicated through it and to the reader about representation and function, especially as counter to other characters? How do the awe of the unreal and the humor of exaggeration mix, and to what purposeful end?

2

Between Life Sized and the Larger than Life

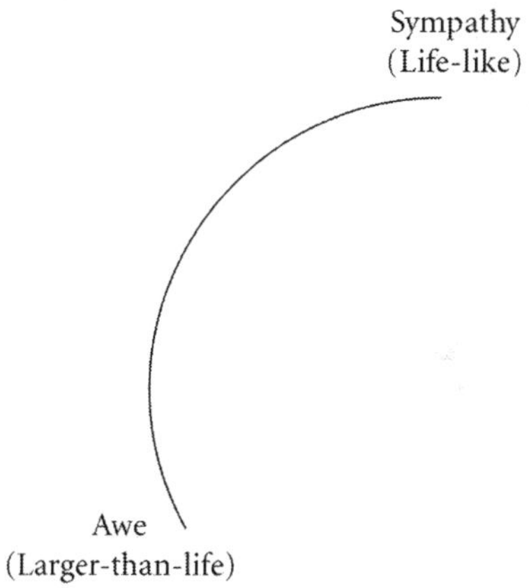

Diagram 2

Between Sympathy and Awe

Suzanne Keen notes that "some varieties of *avante garde* literary practice eschew empathy in favor of shock and defamiliarization" (79), but it is the "circulation of sympathy through author, reader, real world, and text [that] still underwrites most of the boldest claims for the consequences of reading and writing" (90). Rather than think of art's function as either defamiliarization or familiarization, we can see in techniques of characterization in literature for the young a purposeful give and take between the two. For instance, Randi Dickson observes that the pleasurable monster, the monster whom the young are meant to enjoy, must simultaneously attract and repel the reader. The repulsion comes from the degree to which the character is unreal, awesome, awe-full; the attraction comes from the recognition of its reality, the degree to which it warrants sympathy and even empathy—its relative likeness to ourselves. Grover of Sesame Street fame is the unwitting eponymous character of a story called *The Monster at the End of This Book*, in which he fears meeting a monster at the end of the book; he is a monster who fears monsters. He is monstrously human; humanly monstrous. We share his fear, but we are not as afraid for him as we would be if he were human like us and awaiting a monster. There is a rhetorical balance between his likeness to us and his difference from us. I want to consider that space between the unreal and real, between the larger than life and the life sized through which children's authors take child readers. Between the possible character and the impossible character, we find a lot of real estate, and there are many degrees of difference in the distance between the two. There is always a character who seems more or less sympathetic than another, so the line is an assemblage of individual characters that are themselves moving one way or another along that line over the course of a story or a series of stories, or maybe just in contrast to some other character in that story. Sometimes characters become more real, as Coraline's mother does in *Coraline*, and sometimes they become less, like Coraline's Other Mother.

I start with the representational or lifelike, and I position it at the top of the dial I offer because the "real" is the basis on which we *feel* character, whether or not we're entirely sure what that means. I believe that it is the first measure we apply to character, and a character is what it is by virtue of the degrees of distance it is from the lifelike. When an author offers us a character, we gauge its relative position to ourselves (the most real thing possible, after all), including by demographics, disposition, and experience. The most "real" character creates a rhetorical demand for sympathy, or even empathy (identification through recognition). From there, an author can modulate (or "dial") character toward smallness or largeness and, regardless of the direction chosen, lessen the author's rhetorical request that we sympathize with that character. As the author modulates or dials character toward either exaggeration or impossibility, the reader moves from empathy to sympathy to pity, and if it goes too far, to an indifference that can result in complete detachment.

Seeing or not seeing ourselves in character has implications for how we recognize humanity and then employ books for the purpose of multiculturalism, for instance. Authors create empathy when they invite us to feel what a character feels, either because they count on reader recognition or because they forge a connection by offering detailed, vicarious experience, and it's worth knowing when it's one or the other. Authors can invite us to identify with characters even when they place characters at opposite ends of the continuum between real and unreal. Authors invite identification through either empathy or desire, or, in other words, through recognition or projection. Recognition happens when we already see ourselves or the humanity in the character through quantifiable or qualitative means. I can see as the character sees because I recognize in him or her quantitative or qualitative similarities to myself or people I know. Quantitative or demographic connections for me might include the fact that the character is part of a large family, is from the East Coast, or is a brown-haired, brown-eyed, white male. Qualitative connections might be our shared feelings of anxiety about heights, an appreciation for the driest of humor, a preference for cold weather, and an unapologetic love of semicolons. Identification, however, can also be a matter of *projection*. I can be invited to and seize a relationship with a character for its attractiveness that may have little to do with me either qualitatively or quantitatively. This invitation is manifest through costume play that indicates admiration for the power of an unreal character, either hero or villain. This is wish-fulfillment desire: projecting yourself on to a being grander than yourself or others around you—perhaps even unreal altogether. It is when we—readers, after all, an audience most likely to revere writers—project ourselves onto Jo March for her feverish dedication to writing. We say, "I am like Jo March" as a speech act, a declaration, a plan. Saying so makes it so. In an extreme case, it is when you draw a lightning bolt scar on your forehead or put on a suit with a big lightning bolt on the chest. Of course, the degree to which a character might be larger than life, awesome, aspirational, impossibly bad, even, is also likely to hold us apart from it, to create repulsion or worship. When Robin McKinley's Beauty/Honour is met with the transformed Beast, an impossibly handsome specimen of man, her first response is to say, "I can't marry you" because, well, "look at you" (241), by which she means that he's too gorgeous for someone like her with such low self-esteem. She had been willing to marry him when he was monstrous, as she believed herself to be. When he shows her that she has also transformed into a real beauty over the last seven months (there are no mirrors in the Beast's castle, after all), she is surprised but also relieved. The distance is removed; they can relate and therefore become related. Beauty could not, or would not, project herself onto the character of "princess," but she was able to move forward as his bride once it was no longer aspirational but entirely reasonable. Water has found its own level. This is the rhetorical offering authors make to readers: offer empathy or aspiration, and we'll see what works.

Cinderella and Beauty as seen in folktale actually provide complicated cases of identification, not least of which because they are fairytale characters and more what Maria Nikolajeva would describe as semiotic rather than mimetic in function (*Rhetoric* 282). Perrault's character Cinderella, Disney's professed model for the 1950 film, is made both aspirational (identification through projection) and an object of empathy (identification through recognition). She is high-born (projection) and thrust into tough circumstances (recognition). She is beautiful but made common. She is deserving based on birth but achieves success through debasing herself through obedience. Because she does not scheme but is cheated from her desire to attend the ball, she is deserving, as are we, after all. Most ironically, she does not seem especially to desire her good fortune but has it given her, and we want it for her for this very reason. This last point is key for

Beaumont's, McKinley's, and Disney's respective Beauty characters. She is the child who is good in the grocery store by not asking for candy who is then given candy as a reward for not asking for candy. She is given that for which she expresses no desire, but we know in our hearts that she does desire. She must. *We* desire it, after all. On the other hand, the child who expresses desire for candy is not to have it. It's shameful to show that desire so openly or to acknowledge what is your due. Beauties are not to acknowledge their beauty (making them both impossible subjects of projection and yet like us for their belief that they are nothing special). We want them to have the things they didn't value and are asked not to value, and we are allowed to enjoy it for them. They must not see their beauty or special qualities; we see them in the character and insist that they come to see it, making us a sort of valuable helper. Even when Beauty's or Cinderella's sisters are beautiful, they are horrible for their consciousness of it. They are made unsympathetically unreal, monstrous. We need the beautiful or gifted to deny their special gifts, to be humble, or to be truly ignorant of them so they will need us the readers to reassure them that they are indeed special, giving us the dramatic irony that makes us feel better about our position, putting us on equal footing. We say to Harry Potter, another Cinderella, "No, you really *are* a big deal. It's okay. I'm glad I was here to tell you this. I guess that makes me pretty special, too, huh? Just like you, really."[1] Harry gets more complicated and real as he enters adolescence, but when he starts to embrace the idea of his being the Chosen One and tries to fix things by himself apart from his friends, he starts to drift farther toward the impossible. His specialness hasn't changed; his (not our) recognition of it has. We need Ron, an exaggerated boy, and Hermione, an impossible girl, to make him seem more real in the balance. We need that balance between the admirable and common, which is the problem politicians face as they run for office: we want our representatives to be impressive, but they need to be "representative" at the same time. The balance is both necessary and ironic.

Cece Bell's graphic novel for children, *El Deafo*, provides a good case study for how an author modulates character over the course of a book in order to strike a balance between the real and unreal for the reader. The 2014 Newbery Honor book is anthropomorphized autobiographical fiction that tells the story of Cece's grade school years. The story privileges how Cece becomes hearing impaired at a young age and how she copes with that in 1970s Roanoke, Virginia. The book alternatively draws readers in and holds them at arm's length, and the author appeals rhetorically to "insiders" and "outsiders" based on both demographics and relative experience.

Cece Bell explains the rhetorical act of her book in an article by Sarah Bayliss in *School Library Journal*: "My book, in a way, is for hearing people: 'Here's what it's *really* like, here are some pointers.'" The book, Bell says, was originally meant as a "manual about her deafness"; this explains why she doesn't use sign language and other personal things related specifically about her hearing impairment. The book is then for outsiders in large part, and that requires Bell to adapt her story rhetorically. There are sections of the story in which the narrator, young Cece, explains to the reader why she has trouble watching television (72–82). She also shares with the outsider how deafness is not simply a matter to be "fixed" by providing more volume: "Talking more loudly doesn't help" (62–71). The visual metaphor of Cece in a Sherlock Holmes detective hat used on some pages explains the problems of the hearing impaired (30). In all of these cases, there are no indirect or subtle allusions meant for insiders, though that audience will likely still nod in recognition and appreciate this validation. Rather, the author offers language and visual depictions for the outsider who doesn't know this world and who is given some vicarious experience in order to make the character more sympathetic to that outsider. Bell also includes information for the reader who is "outsider" in a more common way—the child who needs glasses. The character Cece is made more *typically* different in this way, which provides some identification through recognition to counter to the more unusual circumstance of being a severely hearing-impaired child. By making the story in part about a more common disability, it includes more readers who can draw the character closer to themselves, which makes them more sympathetic and willing to handle the vicarious issue of hearing impairment.

To go a step further in terms of inclusion and offering recognizable character issues, Bell's editor urged her to include more about friendships and school life (Bayliss), which ultimately changes the ways the book functions rhetorically. What might have originally been a story about a deaf child for hearing children becomes the story of a child who goes about an otherwise "normal" life while incidentally hearing impaired, so this story is rhetorically varied. The child reader who is at once an "outsider" regarding hearing impairment is an "insider" as it relates to sleepovers, relationship trouble, enduring the eternal horrors of gym class, and dealing with parents and siblings. While Cece's problems with hearing impairment and glasses are by different degrees alienating, her problems handling the social dynamics of school, friendship, and family tensions are more designed to make insiders of outsiders.

Other character dynamics at work in *El Deafo* push and pull the reader, rhetorically targeting other groups of insiders and outsiders. The use of anthropomorphism is interesting metaphorically: all of the characters are rabbits (really humans with rabbit characteristics), which visually and metaphorically emphasizes the special relationship between ears and the issue of hearing loss. The anthropomorphism distances the reader with fantasy characterization, but then there is the use of the unreal characterization of herself in the form of a superhero that actually serves as a way to make Cece more sympathetic. While the superhero character El Deafo is a form of projection, wish-fulfillment identification that she imagines, it is not the reader's projection, and most readers will not see El Deafo (basically CeCe in a cape) as an object of identification through either recognition or projection. While the alter ego El Deafo enables the character Cece to project heroism where there might be seen disability, the author Cece invites the reader to sympathize with her in that process. The danger, of course, is that this rhetorical invitation will result in reader pity or even disapproval of what might be considered escapism.

• • •

Character typology is not new, obviously. In children's literature, Maria Nikolajeva's *The Rhetoric of Character in Children's Literature* is the first and last word on that subject. In this case, however, it is

Northrop Frye's scale of character type that is useful for my purposes. While he doesn't address it as a rhetorical process, the scale of character worth or value corresponds to the space between what I'm calling lifelike and larger-than-life characterization. Frye's work is, in part, an attempt to differentiate character—especially protagonists—as a way to understand mode in particular: Romance, Tragedy, Comedy, and Irony. In *Anatomy of Criticism: Four Essays*, Frye offers us a vertical line of character merit, which is not the same thing as a measure of empathy or identification, though it's clearly related. While my concern is the degrees of closeness to which an author draws a child reader, Frye's concern is with the degrees of admirability a character offers, and his most admirable are the least like us.

The distinctions Frye makes between characters results in a continuum that is more a set of stratified distinctions, a vertical line of value. At the top is the mythic. This character is supernatural, better and different by kind from humanity. This character is superior to her surroundings and other characters. Lisa Sainsbury explains that "the most common way of explaining evil in children's literature is as a supernatural force that must be vanquished for the sake of good" (66), so it is a way of simplifying texts. Placed upon what I consider a more horizontal line of degree, it occupies the extreme end of the larger than life. The romantic character is next in Frye's hierarchy.[2] This character blends the supernatural with the human—the demigod figure in literature who participates in both worlds but is still superior to her surroundings. If the mythic character is divine, the romantic is "merely" legendary. Maria Nikolajeva positions Harry Potter in this place (*Rhetoric* 32), and author Rick Riordan pushes his character Percy Jackson in this category. Next down the ladder is the "high mimetic" or superior imitation of humanity. This character is superior by degree to most other humans but is still human. This is the subject of the tragic and epic story for Frye. Nikolajeva argues that "high mimetic characters are supposed to serve as models not only for other characters in the story but for the readers as well. In children's fiction, such characters are used for educational and didactic purposes" (Rhetoric 33).[3] What Frye deems "low mimetic" would be what I call sympathetic or lifelike. This is the character for whom identification of recognition is likely highest. This character is us, or me, or an identifiable you who is among us as equals. Frye would have this character be the subject of comedy, a conservative mode in which story reifies current systems. Frye goes a step lower than lifelike to reach the basement of his hierarchy of character. The ironic character is base. We look down upon him. We pity him. While I want us to think of the movement of character between the real and unreal as a movement of empathetic distance, Frye sees a clear hierarchy of admiration that bottoms out with pity.[4] There is no movement or modulation of character in Frye's model—the character is fixed in the hierarchy. A horizontal line of degree between the unreal and real acknowledges change while also removing the necessary preference or value of character. Frye's model validates the unreal. Critics who advocate for a "growth" model for character value the move toward the real or sympathetic. I contend that neither the move toward the unreal (gaining larger-than-life status) nor the move toward the real (gaining sympathy and recognition) should be seen as growth or improvement. Each shift is a rhetorical modulation to achieve an effect in the reader.

While it may seem obvious that character is a function and construct, we are still confronted with the language of "growth" as it relates to a character's development, whether we're talking about how a character acts morally in a way different than before, how they have matured, or how they have become dynamic or rounder. It is an understandable tendency to talk about characters as though they are people who have lives outside of the text, but we shouldn't.[5] This growth is even seen as a prerequisite for genre: Karen Coats observes that "the idea of a character arc that mimics the enlargement of perspective and the acquisition of a more complex capacity for emotion is so pervasive as to almost seem a requirement of serious realistic fiction for teens" (Bloomsbury 194). Roberta Seelinger Trites observes that "the idea of growth—the investigation of which characters have developed and which have not—is one of the most common principles in the story of children's and adolescent literature" (*Disturbing* 10). We demand that our young adult (YA) novels have an element of what Trites contrasts as either *entwicklungsroman* (a story in which a character changes) or *bildungsroman* (a story of maturation into an adulthood of some definition). That she makes this distinction is important because books that simply show change in character, though this typically implies improvement, keep us focused on change of function in and for the narrative rather than on some sort of growth. In Trites's configuration, adolescent fiction is about power relations, and change is key to that. Trites asks, "What children's book *isn't* about growth?" (10). It might be more accurate to say that all children's stories involve character change; growth is a conclusion we come to about that change, and it's always just a judgment about whether it's change we approve of (whether it happens in a short time or in the process of aging and "maturity") as opposed to change that is meant to achieve a rhetorical effect in the reader. Change, especially in the space between lifelike and larger-than-life characters, is a matter of rhetorically encouraging reader empathy or not. We tend to believe that empathy is a product of character growth rather than a rhetorical manipulation to feel a certain, changed way about a character. Trites observes that Max from Sendak's *Where the Wild Things Are* grows (10), but what he does is change, and we find that change—especially adult readers—gratifying. We approve of his return home. His smile at the end makes us smile, but more important, his removal of his hood moves him from animal to little boy, and we can sympathize or empathize or even identify with him. Is it necessarily growth to want to come home? What Sendak does at the end is dial Max from larger than life (King of the Wild Things) to lifelike (Max) through the use of pictures, and it's a timely rhetorical move that has us happy and sympathetic to Max at the end. Trites acknowledges this problem with growth as a literary measure in contemporary children's fiction herself when she claims that "the narrative of growth in postmodernism thus becomes constituted as an acceptance of one's cultural habitat rather than serving as a narrative about transcendence or separation. The postmodern awareness of the subject's inevitable construction as a product of language renders the construct of self-determination virtually obsolete" (*Disturbing* 18). Characters can't ever be self-determining any more than teen narrators written by adults can be seen as authentic.[6] Trites ultimately pulls the notion of growth out of an organic, Romantic context by pointing out that "once protagonists of the YA novel have learned to negotiate discursively their place in the domination-repression chain of power, they are usually depicted as having grown, satisfying the conventions of the *Entwicklungsroman*" (*Disturbing* 52). We must recognize this rhetorical manipulation by the author to satisfy both convention and reader. The "growth" of character is an expectation of genre as well as reader, and it's achieved through modulation of sympathy and approval rather than through any set of values being lauded. We see this break down when we see Caddie Woodlawn give up her adventurous ways and decide to be a proper young lady since that is the gender and age expectation of her parents and the society both of the setting and the publication. Today we see Caddie's decision potentially as a shame. She is less sympathetic, less the character we have come to know. The value is dated, so the rhetorical gesture fails. Caddie has never "grown"; she has been modulated. Her story as a child protagonist is over, and this modulation marks that. "Growth" has often been gendered: the boy grows to become larger than life and is modulated toward heroic unreality, while the girl grows to become wife in the home and is modulated toward sympathetic domesticity, the mother that we know. *The Secret Garden* is a prime example of this: Colin's narrative arc is toward vibrant manhood and lordship, while Mary has been developed merely to become a tool for his ascendance. Neither is growth so much as a synchronized manipulation of characters to facilitate the new story and new emotions attached—a shift from Mary's story to her role as helper in Colin's story. When Archmage Ged decides to "go home" at the beginning of Le Guin's *Tehanu*, it was seen as a diminishment rather than growth by readers of the original Earthsea series, for instance. Le Guin was making Ged domestic, sympathetic, without magic, and that had different rhetorical effects on readers.[7] Modulation can become dated because rhetorical efficacy is also contingent on the context of culture.

It's worth considering that there's a difference between having a character begin as larger than life and then "diminishing" her as opposed to beginning a character as identifiable and then "enlarging" her. A character who becomes more life sized as we read is in the process of earning sympathy, and we are being asked to believe in and appreciate a transition from the grandiose (whether good or bad) to the real; a character who is given an unreal backstory has already had sympathy and adds grandeur that doesn't sacrifice the sympathy. Ironically, the real time and development is the same, but the emotional requests of and effects on the reader are very different in story time.[8] In other words, two characters may end up in the same place between life sized and larger than life, but we think of them differently depending on from which direction they've come. There is a qualitative and affective difference between moving from life sized to larger than life as opposed to moving from large to real; in the former case, the character is already sympathetic and made larger than life, so there is the sense that "one of our own" has achieved something, has made a jump toward grandeur. We "knew them when," we might think. We can either be glad for them or remind them of where they come from and what they were ("remember that you're just Jenny from the block!"). In the latter case, the character has to attain a sense of humanity—a softening. It's the Velveteen Rabbit effect—we have an increased sympathy for the rabbit that is made "real," after all. So again, two different characters might end up roughly equal parts real and unreal, but it is the movement from one direction to the other that dictates our feelings about them and emotional connection to them.

Moving toward the Grandiose

The move toward largeness is a move made to bolster character gravitas. The character can be shown to shift over story time, or that larger-than-life quality can be achieved quickly through some revelation, usually by using analepsis or backstory, which I'll discuss at length. However it is handled, the move toward the unreal is a move away from reader recognition, so it is important for the author to consider the rhetorical implications for unmooring a character from the real and having it drift toward the unreal. It's usually the case that the character began its construction as more sympathetic in order to carry that quality with it as it becomes more unreal. If the author wants the character ultimately larger than life, it sometimes pays to start it closer to human experience to establish a sympathy that will trail into the unreal. It's a move that drags humanity toward greatness. Such a modulation also suggests to the reader the possibility of her making a similar transformation. "This is a possibility for you," the narrative tells the reader. You can travel from the real and ordinary into the limelight.

The rhetorical shift of a character toward greatness is a trustworthy narrative move. It could be argued that this is a cultural favorite. This is the "local-kid-makes-good" story in which a character begins designed as highly sympathetic and perhaps qualitatively or quantitatively identifiable and is modulated toward the larger than life through a number of devices. The humility of that character becomes a lauded quality once he or she has made it to a more unreal, larger-than-life status, whether in fantasy or realism. Unlike Harry Potter, who is a Cinderella for starting off advantaged only then to be knocked down a peg by life, these characters begin humble and sympathetic. Ponyboy Curtis from *The Outsiders* is a typical model.[9] Ponyboy's character not only is down-and-out, but he's an especially sensitive and sympathetic kid who seems destined for an unremarkable life. After he and Johnny save the children from the church fire, he is hailed as a hero, and his home life and social life stabilize. We have hope for him as a writer and student with a much more upward trajectory than when the novel started. He goes from down-and-outer to hero with prospects, and all rather suddenly, like Charlie Bucket in *Charlie and the Chocolate Factory*. These heroes are made—or, rather, revealed—by their circumstances. They are shown relatively late in the novel to be made of the Right Stuff by the author rather than beginning as characters of whom we are in awe. Jonas from *The Giver* becomes, through his development of empathy and righteous indignation, a character capable of burning the system to the ground. He is on a slow boil to heroism. The novel moves Jonas from "normal kid" to special as the next Receiver of

Memory. As he trains for what would have set him above and apart from his peers, he chooses heroism over prestige when he leaves the village with the baby Gabe who is scheduled for euthanasia. In *The City of Ember*, Lina and Doon become sleuths who suss out the escape path from Ember that enables their society to survive; they are modulated from forgettable, real kids to saviors. Modulation from life sized to larger than life that is a late or slow revelation acts as a sort of reward to reader and character alike. The reader has grown to care about a character who seems normal, unremarkable, like the reader but who later is revealed to have the sort of character that is aspirational as well as inspirational. This sort of shift often happens as the culmination of a long-developing problem, such as bullying. For instance, at the end of Meg Medina's *Burn Baby Burn*, Nora finally stands up to her brother and reports his violence and arson to the police, making a new life for herself possible. A character "finally" finds the nerve, the desperation, or the will to rise above. Sometimes it's just the discovery of talent or magic, as in Dahl's *Matilda*. The author provides the reader a sense of relief. It might be that a competition, award, or publication has come late to validate a character's hopes, and we hope and celebrate with them. This might be Jo March finally publishing a story in *Little Women* or Georgia from Jen Bryant's *Pieces of Georgia* receiving a scholarship at the end of the story.

A particularly effective means of modulating a character so that it gains unreal qualities without much set-up is the use of a portal narrative. Unlike the slow-cook stories discussed above, the portal narrative introduces the shift from real to unreal with the force of sudden and surprising revelation. By "portal," I mean the movement from one chronotope (or unified time-place within a story) to another. This is so common a move in children's literature as to be almost a defining characteristic. The home-away-home movement in children's books has been discussed by many critics, and it isn't restricted to fantasy, though it is a favorite tool in that genre.[10] This Odyssean pattern is seen in children's narratives that employ the hero's journey, large and small—from traveling to Narnia to defeat a White Witch to going to Terabithia to pretend life is better than it really is. The portal narrative is almost always used to make a relatively real character—one built for identification through recognition and sympathy—more unreal in ways that imbue it with grandeur. There are exceptions, of course, but they prove the rule. Gulliver does travel to Brobdingnab, after all, but when *Gulliver's Travels* is converted into a children's book, it's his journey to Lilliput that is featured on the cover, not his journey to Brobdingnab. Diana Wynne Jones' *Howl's Moving Castle* seems to diminish and make real the character of Howl by showing him to be the mere mortal Howell Jenkins from Wales; it's easy to see that from his character's perspective, his Wizard Howl identity is his portal narrative identity—one that magnifies him. Sophie's world, a fantasy chronotope of the medieval type, sees Wales as the "fantasy" portal destination. For the most part, portals provide a quick means to take a character who is seen by the reader to be unremarkable but sympathetic and give them unreal qualities. These are often "chosen-one" narratives in which the otherwise real and sympathetic character is a pretty big deal once through to a different chronotope—like Harry Potter, the Pevensie children, Katniss Everdeen, Coraline, Dorothy Gale, and Max (the wild thing). In each of these cases, the children become more than they were almost instantly upon arriving to the secondary world, and often come back to their own worlds more than they were when the left, invested with honor and imbued with confidence. It is only after defeating the Other Mother in the portal world that Coraline chooses to correct the adults who mistakenly call her "Caroline" in her world. She will no longer suffer that indignity of having her unique identity unrecognized. Again, this isn't limited to fantasy, and in realism this chronotopic shift can be an exercise in wish fulfillment, as in *The Prince and the Pauper* and *The Princess Diaries*, or an opportunity to find a place of refuge to grow and prepare better to be in the world, as in *Slake's Limbo* or *Bridge to Terabithia*. The portal narrative provides a modulation of character that doesn't depend on either long and causal development or a potentially implausible epiphany. The character is suddenly displaced, and that displacement provides the conditions for modulation that staying in the original setting—a setting in which they had been ordinary or even marginal—won't allow as dramatically or easily. In this new place, the character was always different and unreal, and often that arrival was prophesized. The arrival of the character on the threshold of the portal is all that is necessary for modulation. As in the general modulation of real to unreal, the portal narrative holds out hope for the reader that in some circumstance apart from their own, they too may be special, and quite suddenly at that. All it might take is a tornado, a wardrobe, a fall down a rabbit hole, a letter from Hogwarts, a subway tunnel, or a patch of isolated Virginia woodland to make it happen. While most other characters in the home world don't know of the heroism of the returning hero, the reader knows and shares this triumphant (if secretive) homecoming with the character. Terry Pratchett's Tiffany Aching thinks to herself on her way home (and not even her first unheralded return from a place of trial and testing): "Why do you go away? So that you can come back. So that you can see the place you came from with new eyes and different colors. And the people there see you differently, too. Coming back to where you started is not the same as never leaving" (*A Hat Full of Sky* 359). Indeed not. "'I've come back!' she announced to the hills. 'Better than I went!'" (360). It takes a separation from her setting to make it possible. The list of portal modulations is too long to share, but it's worth noting that some of the most significant characters in the most successful children's books are modulated in this way, so there is something to be said about how authors must perceive the rhetorical effect.[11]

Yet another technique other than the "slow-burn" modulation or the introduction of portals is the use of back story. "Back story," Marius Hentea explains, "instead of being a peripheral concern, directs and guides readings. Back story does more than simply make novels comprehensible" (349). Hentea goes on to argue that "back story plays an important and complex role in defining and deepening fictional worlds" (361) and altering character function, and these two things can be mutually exclusive. Eleanor Henderson points out that we "sometimes [. . .] conflate this term with *flashback*, but they're not quite the same thing," and describes flashback as more scenic while backstory is more summative (24).[12] Rather than distinguishing the two along the lines of summary and scene, it may be more useful to contrast them by function. Flashback is about direction; backstory is about content. In any case, it's worth asking about the need to use either at all. Why tell stories out of order? Folktales don't typically do this. In folktales we know what we need to know about characters from the start, and it doesn't change. Our emotions are rhetorically set at the start—we are made to like *her*, distrust *him*, suspect *them*. In a genre like the novel in which character function changes over the course of the story, we are manipulated in other ways. Can a story work without backstory? Yes, if by "work" we mean "is it plausible and clear." But backstory isn't simply narrative play with time, it is a manipulation by the writer of the emotional distance between reader and character. The writer has a reason for wanting you to change your mind about a character. That doesn't happen as well or as quickly in a chronological telling.[13]

Joyce Finn describes backstory as a sort of earned exposition introduced when the intensity of the narrative has calmed, and we have time to listen: "When floodwaters are high, we don't stop to ruminate about the meaning of life—we bail. Reflection, looking back, comes only after the last puddle is squeezed up, the dog calmed, and the carpets drying in the sun" (57). Such a move has a distancing effect on the story since it is a form of interruption. She claims that "it muddies the forward progression and keeps readers from becoming involved and engaged" (57). We are pulled out of immersion. But it isn't necessarily a distancing tool for character. That story interruption might make us feel closer to the character, however; it's the writer's calculated trade-off.[14] A question an author must consider is whether the interruption is worth whatever is achieved in character manipulation. Backstory is an interruption of narrative flow and immersion that can exacerbate distancing by also distancing us from character.[15] This has a doubly distancing effect, then. Instead of focusing on positive or negative distancing, though, I want to consider how characters are made more real or more unreal, which is related to but not reliant on how we like or dislike character. Sometimes a character is made distant from us simply to make them larger than life after an initial grounding in sympathetic reality. In other words, we learn later that the once-believed normal character is actually a big deal. The backstory is a revelation of awe, a supersizing of the character that was initially established and grounded in our sympathy.

Characters, minor or major, can be made "big deals" late in the narrative in order to provide either explanation to the larger plot or increase our sense of wonder of a certain character. In *Number the Stars*, Lowry provides a backstory for both Annemarie's sister Lisle and her fiancé, Peter. Instead of being the victims of a simple car accident, as we and Annemarie have been led to believe, we find out from Annemarie's father at the end of the narrative that they had been targeted by the Nazis for their work in the underground. They weren't just in a car accident; they were run down by the enemy. Loss has been ennobled at the end of the narrative. Lisle's death had been important in the narrative to allow Ellen to take her place as the third sister when the Nazis came calling, but now it has been used to ennoble not only the lost sister but also the family's role in defying the Nazis. This simple backstory amplifies our emotional response at the story's end, whereas it might have been either learned earlier in the story and dissipated emotionally over the reading or never used at all since it isn't essential to the narrative. Lowry's backstory creates more emotional bang at the end of an already emotional conclusion.

Backstory still serves to change our relationship to character even when the story demands that backstory for narrative sense. The character Mandy in *Ella Enchanted* has a backstory that changes the way the narrative can proceed and provides hope after we feel as though the story can't progress. When Ella learns that Mandy—the castle cook—is actually her fairy godmother, Ella has hope that she can gain contact with the fairy Lucinda in order to convince her to remove her "blessing" spell of obedience or, at the least, stop cursing future children with idiotic "blessings." We learn that Mandy has been fairy godmother to Ella's family for generations, but we learn this only when her status as fairy can provide a new narrative direction. It's less true to say that it's revealed since it isn't actually true until the writer makes it so; it's introduced, not revealed. Characters don't have real histories, so the revelation of history always serves the present narrative moment. Mandy becomes more than she was and opens the narrative to new possibilities simply with the introduction of a backstory. She was already sympathetic if not pitiable in her station, but now the character has gained new grandeur. When in *Tuck Everlasting* Winnie Foster is kidnapped by Ma Tuck and Jesse Tuck, she and we have no understanding yet of why they had abducted her. Their backstory—a seemingly fantastic story of a fountain of youth—takes an otherwise ordinary (albeit kidnapper) family and makes them mythic figures: the family who can't die. It is their backstory that gives their lives both pathos and ethical significance. When Ma kills the man in the yellow suit, she is saving not only Winnie but, arguably, the world. Their backstory provides justification for what has had no justification. The author has reassured the reader that the family is to be trusted. In Roald Dahl's *The Witches*, the grandmother's revealed backstory as a retired witch hunter makes it possible for the boy and the grandmother to thwart the witches' diabolical scheme to turn all English children into mice, and she has become something larger than life, though we could argue a loved granny is hard to enlarge.[16]

The above are secondary characters, but main characters are changed through backstory as well. Saaski in Eloise McGraw's *The Moorchild* is one example. This is an example of backstory that not only makes the story possible but also changes the reader's connection to character. After growing up as "freaky odd" in her village and teased by her peers for her strange and different ways, she and we learn together late in the narrative that she is actually a changeling. Known as Moql back in the fairy mound, she is half fairy and half human (the result of a human being lured into the local fairy mound a few years earlier). Deemed insufficiently fairy to be of use to the moorfolk, she is made a changeling. This moves her story from that of a normal and sympathetic target of bullying to something more. Not only is she verified as magical rather than simply an odd human, but she becomes heroic in her own successful quest to rescue her adoptive parents' real child from the mound—something only she can do. After retrieving the child and returning it to its (her) parents, Saaski/Moql lights out for the territories with her friend Tam, another misfit, though of a more conventional type: he's a musician. While the story of a misfit child leaving trouble and making her way in the world is a story worth telling, the changeling backstory both pushes Saaski's character into the unreal and makes possible her heroism. She begins with our sympathy, which she keeps, and becomes a magical hero as well.[17]

Another main character who moves from life sized to larger than life by use of backstory is Will Stanton in Susan Cooper's *The Dark Is Rising* sequence, though this backstory is introduced early in the narrative. The establishment of Will as a boy in a large family waiting impatiently for both snowfall and Christmas to come is enough to mark him as sympathetically real. He, like his brother James, is unnerved at the skittish behavior of the animals and the attack of a strange man by rooks. We are invited to identify with Will's unease at the frightening and seemingly unreal things going on, so the invitation to connect with him is made. Cooper only then, though shortly thereafter, has Will's identity as one Old One revealed to him and us, and he's as much in denial as we expect from characters who believe themselves to be ordinary only to be informed by some unreal messenger that they are not. We learn Will's story as he learns it, and our sympathy for and awe of him are entwined. The character who begins real only to be move toward the unreal approximates the experience of our discovery of our own grandeur. This has happened to Saaski, to Will. They were real and normal like me. They have to wrestle with the news of their specialness. There is a weight that is imposed on them and us. After having been invited to see a character as real, their unreality is felt by the reader more keenly.[18]

There's a much later reveal through backstory in Robin McKinley's *The Blue Sword*. Angharad ("Harry") Crewe, an orphaned noblewoman of the Homeland, goes to distant Damar to be near her brother. While there, she is kidnapped by Damarians and learns their ways unnaturally quickly and proficiently, especially combat. She and we later learn her backstory that makes her negotiation of Damar and their people so facile: she has royal Damarian blood on her mother's side, and the "kelar"—or magic innate to royalty of Damar—is present in her also, enabling her to become adept as both a warrior and healer. The backstory, while having a story function, also moves the character from Homelander orphan to someone both royal and destined to battle greatness like her distant grandmother, Aerin. It is one of many types of backstory that reveals to either character or reader that the character is really royalty. *The Princess Diaries* are an obvious example of this. A young girl is established to be ordinary, likeable, even a bit out of step with her peers, and the revelation of royal blood moves the character from real to unreal, dragging our sympathies along. This is Percy Jackson's story in the series by Rick Riordan. He is believed to be dyslexic, but he is more supernaturally fitted to read ancient Greek as a Greek demigod, it turns out. It is that movement from ordinary to extraordinary through the revelation of backstory that, in fact, works so well upon readers who identify with the real and are given the wish-fulfillment dream that they, too, may be undiscovered royalty. Part of what is important in this rhetorical move is that the character is not only sympathetic to the reader to begin with but is admirably in denial about their royal inheritance. Writers who make the character move from real to unreal are served by making the character so "down to earth" that they refuse at first to believe it and are vaguely disturbed by it. We, the excited readers, are then able to be excited for the character for whom we reassure ourselves that it's a good thing. "No, be excited! We, er, *you* deserve this!" Their reticence is endearing, and it's only the use of backstory that makes it work.

Another of Robin McKinley's acclaimed novels, *Beauty*, provides a backstory that happens about as late as it can in a narrative. In this case, the backstory dramatically changes the "unreal" status of one main character for the benefit of the other. Ironically, it isn't a backstory that makes the story possible but rewards our protagonist by making another story happen—a story that was going on all along without Honour's or our knowledge, presumably. It's a character backstory that revises the story we're being told—makes it an alternative narrative. By the time Honour ("Beauty") has agreed to marry Beast at the end of McKinley's novel, we have built up enormous sympathy for her over the course of hundreds of pages. We are, through this novelization of a marriage tale, given a love story that demands that we see a love story as plausible rather than simply a wise marriage as Beaumont asks in the fairy tale on which the novel is based. McKinley manages to convince us that this relationship is plausible despite the unreal nature of the Beast. At the end of the novel, the curse—one Honour and we don't know about—is broken, and the backstory and transformation of the Beast into a prince shifts the terms of story.[19] Instead of an unreal monster, Beauty is given an equally unreal prince. Instead of realizing he is worthy of her love, she is confronted with her own unworthiness. Had McKinley not hidden from her character narrator that she has grown tall and beautiful in this castle without mirrors over the past several months, Beauty may not have deigned settle for the Beast, but the revelation that she is also beautiful makes her accept her own worthiness and, as a result, the prince. It's clear that before she sees her transformation, she sees a match with the transformed prince unthinkable. It's a neat double switch that requires both a backstory and a plot trick, but it all at once moves us from one love story to the next—one with two homely people who cherish solitude to one with two beauties who are objects of admiration by royal subjects—and we've taken the great sympathy we've had for Honour into the new reality. We have that unreal character who benefits from the foundation of sympathy we've built. She is no two-dimensional princess but a real girl who has been made larger than life.[20]

The adjustment of character by the author, the modulation of function from the real toward the unreal, is a calculated rhetorical move. The reader has established a sense of recognition, qualitatively or quantitatively, and has been invited by the character and author to have a degree of connection, from empathy to pity, though sympathy would seem to be the minimum goal. Once sympathy has been established, however briefly or deliberately, the author can dial the character toward the unreal. The move in this direction often has the feeling of reward for good behavior (often modesty or enduring a bad deal) or being identified for important work. Once our sympathy has been gained, we are invested in the characters already and cheer them on as they reap rewards or assume important positions. They aren't distant, unreal characters—we've known them. We were there before. In many ways, it's our victory, too. This particular character modulation—perhaps the most common in literature for young people—encourages a combination of identification through recognition and projection. We've seen ourselves (or, if not empathetic, at least a sympathetic character) and watch as the unreal is made possible, confirming that even really implausible dreams or lucky strokes are possible for us.[21]

Moving toward Sympathy

I'd like to continue the discussion of backstory as I move to consider character modulation in the other direction along this continuum between the life sized and the larger than life. As we've seen, backstory is a tool for creating a rhetorical effect on viewers and readers as well as a tool to alter plot; it can be used as a means for creating in a short space or time some sympathy or empathy in the reader for a character that is brought down to earth, made more real, by complicating or softening what might be an unreal persona. The change in direction changes the emotional value of the character; it isn't simply moving from the opposite direction. In other words, moving a character toward the middle doesn't make the emotional experience the same for the reader; it matters from which direction that character has come and how. While the move from the real to unreal grounds the grandeur, provides rewards, and builds heroes, the move from the unreal toward the real becomes one of redemption. It provides a different reconsideration of character. It's the difference between the simple epiphany of empathy seen in Dr. Seuss's Grinch and the empathy *we* are asked to feel for *him* in Ron Howard's 2000 film *How the Grinch Stole Christmas*, in which we are given a lengthy backstory of the Grinch's misplacement by stork and sad childhood in what is clearly the wrong world. The 2000 film version modulates the Grinch's character well before his epiphany, and there's a pity for him not present in Seuss's version. Seuss converts an unreal character through the power of example and his realization that Christmas is "a little bit more." The film explains his anger and complicates his character, but because he begins as unreal (in appearance and attitude), and a nasty unreal at that, he is offered reader forgiveness through backstory, though redemption still only comes through that epiphany about Christmas. Backstories that are entire prequel texts—like those of villains Maleficent in recent Disney films and the Wicked Witch of the West as written by Gregory Maguire in *Wicked*—provide no change of heart that alters their previous story, but like the Grinch's, their respective backstories are explanations that create in us pity or even sympathy. They are made complicated, and their actions are given reasons that are or are not excuses depending on the reader or viewer. The modulations of their characters are emotional revisions.[22]

There are many examples of the character who is grounded, made more real by backstory, and they happen in various degrees depending on the change in emotional connection that the author wants the reader (and other characters) to have with those characters. Mrs. Coulter and Lord Asriel are given what we would expect is emotional grounding in Philip Pullman's His Dark Materials saga when we and Lyra discover through Lord Faa of the Gyptians that they are Lyra's parents. Their motives and devotions become only slightly mitigated, however. Coulter and Asriel are larger than life in their abilities and stations, and they are selfish and unsympathetic characters, even villainous. Mrs. Coulter's desire to save Lyra from intercision (the severing of one from one's daemon) does not soften our emotional connection to her; it's clear that she is not herself an empathetic person but selfish. The other children don't matter to her, as Lyra herself points out. The backstories of Lyra's parents add intrigue and connection among storylines, but they do little to modulate their characters for the reader emotionally. A stronger grounding happens in Diana Jones's *Howl's Moving Castle*, in which we learn by degrees that the Wizard Howl is not so fearsome or unusual. Mostly we learn this by degrees of exposure to our focalizing protagonist, Sophie. Jones introduces the backstory of Howl as Howell Jenkins, a citizen of Wales. In other words, while he is dehorned by degrees over the course of the novel, he is offered up as not terribly unlike the reader as a person born in an average family in Wales, however gifted he might be. He is not only not dangerous to Sophie, but he's one of us—even unlike Sophie, who is a native of the world of Ingary. This is clearly a retelling of the Wizard's story in *The Wonderful Wizard of Oz*, who is a simple balloonist from Omaha mistaken for a wizard upon his arrival in Oz (186). Jones modulates Howl/Howell's character over time and with one last piece of information through backstory so we increasingly have more sympathy and then potentially identification through quantification—he's just a kid from nearby Wales. The Thief Lord, the titular character of Cornelia Funke's novel, turns out to be a bored rich kid who has simply been stealing from his own family. Grandeur turns to pity and then slowly to sympathy.

A powerful example of the use of backstory to dramatically alter a character's emotional meaning for the reader is in Rita Williams-Garcia's *One Crazy Summer*. In this novel, eleven-year-old Delphine and her two younger sisters are sent out to visit their mother, who left them with their father six years earlier and never returned. On page two-hundred-seven of a novel that has only nine pages remaining, the reader and the protagonist, Delphine, are both given Cecile's backstory—a backstory that has the potential to change everything. Up until this point, the reader has been invited to take the side of Delphine's father and paternal grandmother in the account of things, which simply indicates a mysterious and unconscionable desertion by the mother, Cecile. What the backstory tells us is that this was not desertion but escape, and that turns on the question of sympathy. In the space of five pages, we and Delphine are given the revelation that homeless and orphaned Cecile had basically been taken in off the streets at sixteen by Delphine's father and impregnated shortly thereafter, and twice more in four years:

> "Your father found me on a park bench. He and his brother had a nice apartment on Herkimer Street. He fed me. Gave me a bed to sleep on. I hadn't slept on a bed since I was eleven years old and my mother was alive.
>
> "Louis never bothered me. Didn't ask me to do much but cook. Sweep. Wash his clothes." She paused. "I had you the next year." (208)

In that literally pregnant pause, we are told about Cecile's life and the conditions under which she is allowed to stay housed and fed. After the birth of a third child in five years, she leaves. The reader is asked to consider this an escape for the first time, and Delphine has to think more about it, but the seed of doubt has been planted regarding desertion. Cecile's character has been modulated. It now invites sympathy if not merely pity. Some readers will decide that it is enough; others will not, but the gesture has been made by the author to move the reader closer to Cecile at the end of the novel—deferred sympathy.[23] She has moved from the unreal monster who left them to a teenager abducted who finally decides to flee at twenty-one. It makes the family hug at the end of the book plausible for the reader.

Perhaps the best well-known backstory in recent children's literature history can be found in J. K. Rowling's *Harry Potter and the Half-Blood Prince*, the penultimate book in the seven-volume Harry Potter saga. After five-and-one-half volumes of inviting the reader to see Voldemort as diabolical and larger than life, Rowling introduces a backstory that modulates his character for an important emotional effect on the reader. Voldemort's backstory has its plot importance as well. Upon learning of Voldemort's parentage, Harry asks Dumbledore, as we might of Rowling, whether it is "important to know all this about Voldemort's past," to which Dumbledore responds and Rowling implies, "Very important, I think" (215). In any case, when Dumbledore shares more of Tom Riddle's history, Harry is indignant at Tom's mother's actions toward her son, prompting Dumbledore to ask of Harry, and perhaps Rowling of us, "Could you possibly be feeling sorry for Lord Voldemort?" (262). While it served the narrative for us to know only that Voldemort is a powerful dark wizard who has tried and continues to try to kill Harry and impose his will upon the world, now Rowling has decided that we need to feel new emotions regarding Voldemort. The irony is that he—champion of "pure blood" wizards—is himself a "mudblood" sired by a muggle father. That and the fact that he was left an orphan help to complicate his character in ways that seem meant to provoke both disgust as well as a sad pity in the reader. It makes Voldemort smaller and sadder. Rowling dials his character just enough toward pity to take him down a peg rather than foster genuine fellow feeling. His background makes him a hypocrite and cruel by nature from the start. That Harry speaks up about the indignation of his past says much more about Harry than it does Voldemort. Harry feels more than we do, partly because he's had a similar orphaned and abused past, but also because he's "better" than us in admirable ways. Voldemort's backstory, ironically, helps Harry by comparison and through his reaction.

Harry and Voldemort are meant to be compared throughout the series, certainly, and the relationship between real and unreal and the chronological order of the telling are important. Harry's past is given to us early so we can sympathize immediately. He is orphaned and abused but seems, oddly, well-adjusted and normal. He has a tormentor in his cousin Dudley rather than being the one tormenting, as Voldemort does in the orphanage. He doubts his worth and his identity as a wizard; Voldemort believes himself to be special from the start. Voldemort's background is withheld until later, so that we won't begin with sympathy; we get just enough information far enough into the story, so there isn't a risk of developing more than a disgusted pity for him, and this is all about the use and timing of backstory.

• • •

Of course, characters need neither portals nor backstory to be made more real and less unreal. Eschewing these sorts of narrative moves, the author has to communicate the modulation of character over time in the narrative. There are, of course, the occasional sudden transformations, but they are not usually very persuasive. Ah-ha moments are more likely to seem contrived. A well-known visual example in a children's text is the case of the Winter Warlock in the classic Claymation film *Santa Claus Is Coming to Town*. We have what we assume is a long-time evil, larger-than-life wizard literally melting before us, though not in Wicked Witch of the West or Indiana Jones Nazi fashion. This is a good melting (as the Grinch's heart-size increase isn't as deadly as it might look). When Kris Kringle hands the Winter Warlock a toy train, we are given an epiphany—nobody has ever given the Winter Warlock a present (which is its own summative backstory). This act alone shows the immediate melting of the warlock's icy exterior to reveal a nice, frail, old, and less magical white man with better teeth. He becomes more real in a number of ways, then—visually, magically, and demographically common. But unlike the Grinch, whose well-established prejudices are shown late in the narrative to be only partly true, the Winter Warlock is transformed almost as soon as introduced. He has been zapped, and it rings hollow despite our being glad for the change. Some rhetorical modulation necessarily happens over time, for it is hard to make things real but even harder to make others accept it.

The Velveteen Rabbit is perhaps the first character in children's literature one might call to mind when thinking about "becoming real." His becoming scuffed and pitiable is a modulation of sympathy, after all. The character that is new and hard and without emotion is less sympathetic. The move to make him biologically real is a second move toward us. He doesn't become a real boy, as Pinocchio does, another character who is modulated toward the real as a way for us to warm to him. In both the Velveteen Rabbit's and Pinocchio's respective cases, becoming flesh and blood is a reward, and to become more like us as a reward is a highly sympathetic move.[24] In these children's stories, the characters begin as unreal—held at arm's length from both the living world of their stories and the young readers they are offered up to by the author. Over the course of their respective narratives, they must prove themselves worthy to become, well, more like us. They have to earn their heartbeats and breathing. They each are presented with failure—set for burning or consumption by a whale—only to be judged worthy by the fairies who are second cousins to the one that decides that Beauty's Beast is worthy. Whatever else anthropomorphism does, it is a modulation tool moving character closer to or further from us.[25] Andersen's and Disney's respective Little Mermaids, as different as their stories end up, are both seen to have made a preferable transformation from mer-person to person, a move from the unreal or fantastic to the real that the young reader is assumed to find an improvement. In

Andersen's case, it makes the girl eligible for heaven; for Disney, she can get the boy. This is different, after all, from finding the other more sympathetic.

A curious case of anthropomorphic modulation, mentioned in chapter 1 of this book, involves Arthur Read. In Marc Brown's series that features our eponymous character Arthur, there happens a transformation of character that is restricted to the illustrations. While Arthur's manner hasn't changed over the years, his appearance has. In the 1976 debut Arthur book, *Arthur's Nose*, the title points to the problematic proboscis. The cover and interior illustrations show that Arthur is, in fact, an aardvark. His nose is long and troublesome since he lives among other anthropomorphic animals in a world constructed for humans. He is also brown, furry, small-eyed, and about as unlike a human as an aardvark in human clothes can be. By the time we meet Arthur in Brown's 2011 *Arthur Turns Green*, he is, ironically, noseless. He looks like a young Voldemort with unfortunate ears, actually. I can't imagine what contemporary readers unfamiliar with the aardvark Arthur thinks he is. You would never know that he is an aardvark by 2011. He is clearly a furless, white boy with oddly placed ears, no nose, and no hair. The transformation is gradual. In the early years his nose becomes more moose-like, connected to a mouth in a long snout that shortens even more over time. Instead of a story-length modulation, this is modulation that takes over forty books and thirty-five years. It's almost as if Brown regretted using animal characters in the first place and has made them more and more human over time. The characters have been modulated to be more real, although they are rather misshapen people instead of recognizable animals in many cases, so I'm not sure if that goal has been achieved.

The child reader needs to see how the nonhuman, the unreal human, is really worthy of pity, sympathy, and empathy. Writers for children often modulate character to provide the pleasure of ultimate recognition. Even Wild Things can be saved. Max's change of heart leads him back to humanity in *Where the Wild Things Are*, and the story's last page ends with him in his room with his wolf hood removed, finally, and no longer the larger-than-life king of all the Wild Things. He is the most human he's been visually, and as we felt sorry for him that he was lonely for company among the Wild Things, we are relieved to see him home. Monsters can be made like us by creating empathy for their fears. Jessica McCort has it that "some children's and YA texts that appropriate horror, especially those designed for the very young, transform the monster into the protagonist" (12), and that is certainly true of Grover in *There's a Monster at the End of This Book*. His fear of monsters, his horror at running into a monster, makes him real to us.

McCort also points out that faux horror "adopts what has traditionally been found terrifying and adapts it into something to be befriended and desired," and sometimes even funny (13). *Monsters, Inc.*, *Shrek*, and the *Hotel Transylvania* films reverse the roles of monster to empathetic victim of human violence. It is the human who is made less empathetic as insensitive, judgmental, intolerant, and potentially violent. We see this same move in *Charlotte's Web*, a story that opens with the line "Where's Pa going with that axe?" (1) and continues to show the humans as monstrous killers of poor animals, as well as hopelessly gullible. When Fern learns of Wilbur's fate, she exclaims in horror, "Do *away* with? You mean *kill* it? Just because it's smaller than the others?" (1). Wilbur is told by his friends in the barn that "They're fattening you up because they're going to kill you" (49). But even Wilbur—made real to us from the start through this empathy and being turned into a baby by Fern—turns and accuses Charlotte of cruelty and bloodthirst when she shows him how she captures flies. She is made a spider by White, not a person, so she must "make a living" how she is able, but she bemoans her "miserable inheritance" (39). White moves Charlotte toward the real as the book and her selflessness progress—all while not sacrificing her spider nature, which is a neat trick. When she dies alone at the fair, she is fully an object of empathy and yet fully a spider. By the same token, she makes Wilbur increasingly loved as a needy child despite his very piglike nature.

The monster begins as unreal but can quickly or slowly be made real over the course of the story, so it drags the impressive nature of its unreality into the realm of empathy—a powerful combination.

Terry Pratchett's Hiver, found in the Tiffany Aching book *A Hat Full of Sky*, is a monster made real and sympathetic very late in the novel. After terrifying, even possessing Tiffany for much of the novel, it is Tiffany's turn toward rather than away from the Hiver that enables the understanding necessary to free the Hiver and save herself. We are introduced to the Hiver early in the book. It is, like "a swarm of bees. One mind with *thousands* of little bodies" (85). After Tiffany has thrown the Hiver from her body, with the help of the Nac Mac Feegle, she decides to face it and give it what it wants, and that turns out to be its own death. She renames the Hiver "Arthur," giving it a sense of identity and humanity. Once Tiffany—and we—understand that the Hiver is simply afraid and tired of feeling all the emotion in the world around it (for it is, ironically, highly empathetic itself to the point of madness and terror [290]). The Hiver seeks out strong people to find some sanctuary within, for it believes being in a strong person makes it strong, and "When I am strongest, I shall be safe" (180). Tiffany teaches it how to finally die, to be at rest. To do that, we learn, one must be an "I" (311). One must have identity. It is made real enough to be sympathized with, and its journey is complete.

The same move of the protagonist embracing the monster antagonist at the very end is made by Ged at the end of Le Guin's *A Wizard of Earthsea*—also at the very end of a story of pursuit by a monster. Ged turns toward the pursuing Shadow, the formless monster that tries to possess Ged and use him as the Hiver tries to take Tiffany's power. When Ged finally meets and embraces the Shadow, he makes a gesture that all at once—like magic, after all—makes the Shadow as real to us as Ged. Ged calls the shadow "Ged" (194). Of course, Ged himself is a person who is fairly monstrous at his story's start and made real over the course of the series' first book. He is a powerful, impatient, arrogant young wizard who believes himself smarter and more able than his master, Ogion. He releases the powerful shadow from the Drylands (death) in an act of arrogance as he is engaged in a battle of pride with the older student Jasper. Once the shadow is loosed, however, Ged begins to develop humility. As E. B. White takes a risk in making Charlotte a spider, Le Guin risks that we will not want to continue the story of a haughty young man, but the authors make the characters more and more real and sympathetic over the course of their respective stories, and we love these characters all the more for having earned our sympathy over time.[26]

Characters can be modulated between the real and unreal along the different continua of wealth, humanity (in the case of anthropomorphism), magic, age, and others that offer differences of degree that can be changed. Esperanza in *Esperanza Rising* becomes more real when she loses her money because she gains the humility that Ged gains when he loses magic. Both Arthur Read and Pinocchio become more real as each loses his nose. Tenar becomes more real when she loses the authority of being a priestess—an adult role—and becomes a child again. For a character in a children's story to become sympathetic means for her to lose those things that would create awe in the reader. The author demystifies the character, and the reader is made to sympathize with the loss and potentially replaces identification as projection with identification as recognition. The move in either direction is a powerful persuasion to the reader to feel something developing rather than simply being given characters with static and assigned identities.

The space between the real and the unreal may be the most significant axis of modulation for a children's character, but it is by no means the only one. There are important implications for the relationship of both the real and the unreal character as it is modulated with the smaller-than-life character.

3

Between the Life Sized and the Smaller than Life

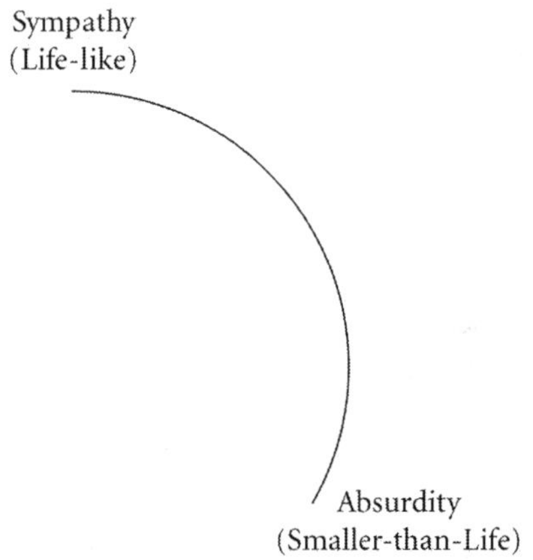

Diagram 3

Between Sympathy and Laughter

Now let us consider the relationship between the "life-sized" character—marked by high degrees of sympathy and identification through recognition—and the "smaller-than-life" character, marked by absurdity and diminishment. The modulation of character between the real and absurd, just like the movement between the real and the larger than life or unreal, is characterized by the distance the author tries to create between reader and character by degrees of sympathy or empathy. In the last chapter, I pointed to how as a character is modulated from reality toward the larger-than-life unreality of the superhero/villain, it becomes potentially an object of identification through projection, a wish-fulfillment character, or an object of intense loathing. As the character is shifted toward the size of life and recognition, we find it more sympathetic. The movement in either direction means trailing qualities from the place from which it started moving: heroes gain sympathy but retain our awe; regular folks gain awe while retaining our sympathy. In contrast, the movement between the real and the absurd or smaller than life is also a matter of distancing, but the "real" becomes the larger expression of character in this dynamic. As a character is drawn, through pictures or words (or both), as folkloric or comic, it is simplified, diminished, or warped into a smaller version of the real. This diminishment is no more a condemnation of character nor an indictment of authorial ability than the enlargement of character is superior to the sympathetic—it's simply another choice available to the author for rhetorical effect. Junie B. Jones isn't a badly made character; she's a character built to create a calculated effect, like any well-made character. She's ridiculous and unbelievable, but she's meant to be. Her construction achieves a rhetorical goal—we feel superior to her and laugh at her, and we find her delightful. Her character is not failed realism. We do not identify with her, however; identification is not always the goal, after all.

The idea that a rhetoric of character could be visualized on a continuum first occurred to me in a class discussion of Junie B. Jones as both character and drawn image. She is not only characterized as exaggerated through dialogue and description; she is drawn that way, too.[1] She is consistently drawn in more exaggerated, indeed cartoonish, ways in contrast to a character like her teacher Mr. Scary or her friend Herb. Tattletale May, however, a character meant to provide a modulated balance, is even more ridiculous than Junie, and illustrations of her are even more exaggerated than those of Junie B. Unlike the range between real and larger than life, the range between the representational and cartoon can be understood pretty well in terms of illustrations.[2] That children's and young adult (YA) literature include picture books, graphic narratives, and illustrated chapter books indicates the extent to which the image, and images of characters in particular, is a paramount consideration in the rhetoric of character. We can see a range of placements from representational to folk-art simplicity and ultimately to the comically exaggerated. The life-sized character is, as discussed in chapter 1, the character who, through physical illustration and/or authorial depiction through prose (description, narration, dialogue), is most sympathetic or even empathetic through our recognition of ourselves in that character (identification through recognition in either qualitative or quantitative measures) or is most realistic and plausible as a representation of others that we can identify as worthy of our sympathy despite some differences. We can accept as "real" or sympathetic in equal measure characters in the genres of realism or fantasy, of course. It doesn't matter if the character is a hobbit; what matters is that the choice of artistic depiction is sending us a message about accepting that character as worthy of sympathy. The school of art chosen, in other words, also acts as a tool of distancing character.

Illustration as Modulation

Perry Nodelman brought to our attention the ways words and pictures work (or don't work) together with his landmark book *Words about Pictures*, so the ideas that pictures contribute different messages than the words, that the relationship between the two is ironic, and that words or pictures can communicate more emotional information are not new.[3] My goal here is to discuss the ways genre, character, and illustration combine as rhetorical tools to modulate distance. In other words, how do authors and illustrators hold readers back or invite them closer through the combination of genre, character, and illustration? Cognitive narratology, reader response, and other affective approaches consider the ways texts play on readers and the sense readers make of texts; I'm more interested in looking at what choices authors and illustrators make in an emotional appeal, in creating intimacy or establishing distance.[4]

It is often a revelation to my students that there are different ways stories might have played out. Part of their development as critical thinkers is to be able to envision the options available to writers and illustrators: the choices made were not inevitable but weighed carefully against alternatives. It is important, for instance, to recognize that stories by David Wiesner are always surreal in content but also always drawn employing realism. Together, they create what Wiesner must hope is a singular emotional experience that is based on a rhetoric of immersion into the unreal. We see in the case of *Tuesday*, for instance, realistically drawn frogs flying through town on lily pads. The narrative asks us to suspend our disbelief regarding flying frogs and bids us to accept it as real through the use of representational illustration, thereby bringing us closer—immersing us—rather than distancing us from it. The surreal is made real. Or we might consider Bernard Waber's two Ira books, both in the genre of realism but illustrated in Waber's signature cartoon style.[5] The action is in a world we know, but characters are exaggerated in appearance, providing distance from the real, so that we have space to laugh at what might otherwise ask too much emotionally of the young reader, making her as sad as Ira at moments. The real is made to a degree ridiculous. Students will see that *Tuesday* rendered in cartoon and *Ira* rendered in realism would create different rhetorical gestures regarding immersion and protection. The style of art isn't simply an indication of the seriousness with which we are meant to take character, then—it is also an indication of the emotional distance created between reader and character. Illustration is a tool for manipulating emotional distance in various ways. The presence of cartoon, for example, might have competing rhetorical intents—it runs the risk of making the content ridiculous rather than sympathetic, but it can simultaneously be used to create safe distance regarding emotionally difficult and serious content. Like all rhetorical choices, there are trade-offs and unforeseen outcomes in their use.[6]

Sometimes character, genre, and school of art line up in terms of distancing. Eve Bunting is a renowned author of social justice narratives for young children. *The Wall*, a story about the Vietnam Memorial, and *Fly Away Home*, a story about homelessness, are illustrated by Robert Himler to represent the characters and their setting realistically, and they are clearly meant to present those characters as highly sympathetic regarding their problems—problems most readers are unlikely to have but with which we are invited to sympathize through three manifestations of realism—character, genre, and illustration. Distance is removed, and the emotional impact is meant to be high. The rhetorical design does not protect the reader but challenges, compels her. We are not to look away. In contrast, Cece Bell's *El Deafo*, another text that tries to raise social consciousness about something not commonly experienced—total hearing loss—invites closeness through the use of the memoir genre, but because it is a graphic narrative that employs animal fantasy and cartoon, it is doubly distancing and perhaps confusing. What is the intended effect on the reader? Bell has reported using rabbits for the metaphoric emphasis on ears, which is clever, but does the semiotic use of character distance us from sympathy? Does cartoon invite us to laugh at what might not be funny? Or do those things create some sort of protection for the reader who might be disturbed by the idea of going deaf? Few of my students comment on the effectiveness of the metaphor much less recognize it right away.

Another straight lineup of distancing employs the unreal. William Steig's *Shrek* is the story of an ogre in an imaginary world drawn in cartoon. We are triply distanced. While Bunting wants us to be immersed and develop sympathy for a problem the reader likely (hopefully) doesn't have, Steig wants us to laugh at something potentially frightening from a safe distance, and Steig must believe that this calls for a rhetorical act that trebles the distance using fantasy settting, impossible character, and cartoon. Anything that draws us even remotely close to Shrek is unacceptable, Steig implies.

Folk art still reduces character to something less real and, arguably, less sympathetic, but folk-art simplification also creates a space for nostalgic projection. We have distancing, but the simplification builds simple and positive emotions uncomplicated by realistic representation. As I discuss above, the use of art can complement more or less realistic language descriptions of character. A character might be built one way with language and modulated in a different direction with art. In a way, a folkloric or naïve depiction of character has the rhetorical effect of understatement. The listener recognizes that there is more to it than what she sees, that there is a reduction of intensity and volume, so to speak. As cartoon exaggerates, folk art understates—but both provide a smaller-than-life character more distant from the realism necessary for sympathy and empathy. The understatement of folk art offers the equivalent of the lack of interiority in character description or development and focuses on the external. The use of folk art has the effect of distancing the reader from the character while simultaneously simplifying them; the simplification can heighten an appreciation for the characters through nostalgia or in the removal of complicated complexity. This is the same thing that happens in prose—the depiction of characters as simple can be purposefully employed to communicate to the reader that there will be no complications or complexities in what amounts to a conservative depiction not only of personality but also of childhood itself: consider Winnie-the-Pooh exhibit A. The visual rhetorical message sent by folk art to the reader is that this character, and likely the narrative itself, will not require a strong emotional connection nor likely the need to identify with the character. We can be touched by folk-art characters, but we aren't invited to connect with them. They are admired at a safe distance. The nostalgia and simple appreciation of Patricia Polacco's characterization in her picture books is especially reliant on folk-art techniques, for example, while her language depictions of them are typically more realistic.

The distancing effect of folk art and cartoon makes those schools of art useful for offering emotional protection. While Eve Bunting's narratives about veterans and homelessness employ representational art to encourage closeness and sympathy in the reader, her book *Smoky Night*—an account of the 1991 Los Angeles riots following the police beating of Rodney King—is rendered in David Diaz's Caldecott Award–winning folk art. The story offers depictions of actual violence, unlike the sedate depictions of Vietnam veterans or homelessness in her other books, so she (the publisher, the artist) employs visual distance. It's a rhetorical choice. So, it's the case that cartoon or folk art is employed to temper connection while still teaching of us about hard things.

Marjane Satrapi's graphic childhood memoir *Persepolis* spares no depictions or descriptions of the horrors and dangers of growing up during the Islamic Revolution in Iran, but the use of minimalistic folk art makes the depictions of character less frightening and demanding for the reader. Does it risk simplifying and therefore distancing the reader from an ethnically and culturally different character, culture, and history? Yes, but it's a rhetorical trade-off. A gamble. Rhetorical choices are always balancing potential effects. Satrapi offers depictions of characters being harassed, tortured, jailed, and even dismembered, but the use of the simple folk art keeps the reality of the horror at bay while still asking the reader sympathy for the people involved, though they remain somewhat unreal. This is also the case in another historical nonfiction text: Robyn Schanzer's historical graphic narrative of the Salem witch trials in *Witches!* Schanzer uses folk-art representations that keep us from being overwhelmed by the imagined point of view of the Puritans regarding the supernatural horrors occurring, so she attempts to put the reader in the buckled shoes of the other. We are asked to empathize with those afraid of witches by being given their perspective and imagined reality, but we are distanced through the style of art. These examples of graphic narratives show the rhetorical calculations authors and illustrators make in sharing nonfiction horrors with young readers, and using the rhetorical gestures of distancing—though words or pictures—is chief among them.

Consider the mixture of distance-modulating rhetorical elements in a few versions of Neil Gaiman's *Coraline*; depending on the version or format you encounter, there is a different rhetorical gesture made. Gaiman has revised many of his texts into multiple formats—going from prose novel to film to graphic novel to picture book—and seems consciously to make different rhetorical gestures each time. There have been several adaptations of the award-winning

2002 novel by Gaiman, including a Claymation film by Tim Burton and a graphic novel by P. Craig Russell.

The 2002 novel is illustrated by Dave McKean, and the images are decidedly surreal. McKean represents Coraline herself as well as the other characters in the novel as warped and unreal. I discuss above the potential disconnect between genre and illustration—as story written as realism might have cartoon illustrations, a tale of fantasy might have representational images. In the case of McKean's *Coraline*, the images parallel the warp of this horror fantasy. Gaiman's tale and McKean's illustrations cocreate a reinforced sense of unreality. McKean's images distance us from while simultaneously reinforcing the sense of warp offered by the story. The collaboration signals from the cover onward that there is something unreal to come, but we will not be asked to immerse ourselves in it entirely. Though Coraline is a potentially identifiable girl who lives in a real Britain, McKean's illustrations of her hold us at arm's length.

Both the Tim Burton film and the graphic novel by P. Craig Russell appeared in 2009, and they offer very different relationships with viewers/readers.[7] While readers of any novel will likely neither notice nor care about new editions of a book that offer only new cover art, fans of the original novel will likely want to see a film or graphic novel adaptation of the novel, so we can assume that readers of the 2002 novel carried McKean's visual images with them to the Burton film and Russell graphic novel, creating a revisionary experience that begins with those original warped, smaller-than-life images. Readers and viewers will also, from 2009 onward, possibly first encounter Coraline as either the movie or the graphic novel and become aware of the McKean illustrations later.

Moving from McKean's illustrated version to the Tim Burton film, fans will shift from one type of smaller-than-life experience to another, though with different effects. In both cases, the consumer is kept at arm's length—in one case with a reinforced sense of surreal detachment, and with the other, a contradictory rhetorical invitation to be amused by Burton's cartoonish depiction of characters, especially the protagonist. McKean's characters are warped to the point that no clear emotion can be read on the face of a character, further insulating the reader from that emotion. The Burton Coraline, however, is very expressive, as cartoons often are, and wears emotion openly but in exaggerated fashion. The character is often depicted as confident; this is undoubtedly meant to reassure the reader/viewer. McKean never offers this reassurance while simultaneously keeping the reader distant from emotion and representationalism. So, both images are distancing, but only one is emotionally reassuring. They are different messages, to be sure, despite both being distancing.

The Russell version of *Coraline* is altogether different. Russell's images offer to the horror-fantasy reader a more immersive experience with the horror-portal fantasy in a text that is verbatim Gaiman's. The cover parallels McKean's cover: we see Coraline holding a candle in the darkness. Russell's Coraline, however, is realistically drawn and clearly nervous, and the real girl is "activated" as a subject of sympathy through realistic, detailed representation to go along with her written depiction. Russell's images are representational renderings of Gaiman's story, and he employs cinematic horror techniques such as the disorienting angles of point of view and close-ups to further disorient the reader while also immersing her in what is happening to Coraline. The rhetorical gesture is not protective but immersive, and it's a radically different invitation than either McKean's or Burton's differently distancing offerings. We see a realistic Coraline in danger in an unreal world made real, and expressing fear and concern throughout the rendering. Russell's Coraline character is the most sympathetic and, in this particular case, most feared for. Gaiman, as corhetor in each of these cases, seems interested in offering readers and viewers differing emotional relationships to his protagonist. Gaiman and colleagues manage to communicate three different emotional relationships to his Coraline through these three different texts.

Author/illustrators offer to the reader cartoonish characters so that we will laugh *at* rather than *with* those characters, and the cartoonish character provides too little humanity for the child reader to feel conflicted about that laughter. The child reader can snort without compunction for she is clearly above, more real, and superior to the character she's exposed to. When a character is built to inspire ridicule, it is rarely modulated to ask for sympathy later. Ethicist and children's author Claudia Mills makes the appeal: "Rather than providing children with vivid (often comic) presentations of prejudice that inspire imitation, we might do better to model more positive ways of interacting with others. We might, that is, do better to write about the world more as we wish it were than as we fear it to be" (*Ethics and Children's Literature* 10). Race's representation through character requires its own book-length study, but if we consider it in terms of the idea of rhetoric, it becomes clear that readers are being asked to conclude things about characters depending on how real or exaggerated they are depicted. In her study of the development of the African American character in American children's books, Mara Hinderer points out that "authors, teachers, and librarians argued that adults had an ethical obligation to provide Black children with more realistic descriptions of children like themselves" (52). The visual depiction of character is a very important part of this work. Celebrated illustrator Jerry Pinkney's work has been admired exactly for how it has ensured that child readers of any race will regard the African American characters he renders. In his many picture books and novel covers, Pinkney makes real and sympathetic the subjects of biography, as in his illustrations of Mary McLeod Bethune in Eloise Greenfield's eponymous title, or fictional and realistic characters, such as his depiction of Cassie Logan on the cover of Mildred Taylor's *Roll of Thunder, Hear My Cry*, or even of folktale legend John Henry in Julius Lester's retelling. His depictions invite the reader to embrace or come close to these characters through his detailed, water-colored realism. E. B. Lewis' depiction of both white and Black children in Jacqueline Woodson's story of segregation, *The Other Side*, invites the reader to sympathize with both Clover, an African American girl, and Annie, who is white, as they sit and talk atop a fence that separates the town and the two girls according to race. In another case of racial representationalism in picture form, Shaun Tan's wordless graphic narrative *The Arrival* tells the story of a man emigrating to another land in order to find work to support his family. The book shows the new land as racially diverse but also, importantly, shows each character through detailed representationalism as a unique and realistic person rather than a simple racial signifier. Tan's choice to make all visual representations of people complicated, unique, and racially varied makes the book about racial diversity without calling to the reader's attention the depiction of race.

Something as minor as a book cover can alter the rhetorical effect of character. In chapter 1, I discussed the shifting of character in the novel *One Crazy Summer* by Rita Williams-Garcia through the use of backstory. It revised the way we see the girls' mother, Celeste, as sympathetic. However, the cover art for various editions and sequel novels depicts the girls as cartoonish, which—as the peritextual element first encountered by the reader—sends a signal of distance, depthlessness, and humor rather than closeness, development, and sympathy. The author's rhetorical use of character has to recover from the reader's initial exposure to the rhetoric of the cover art, which may take several chapters reading into the novel. In other words, the rhetoric of the illustrated cover art serves as misdirection for the author's rhetorical offering of characters as representational, and so the writing modulates the cover art, moving the reader from smaller than life to lifelike.

Ironically, while cartoon is usually guilty of perpetuating exaggerated, demeaning depictions of difference, it can—*because* it is a tool used for creating distance between reader and character—be used as a rhetorical tool for making what might be uncomfortable safer to contemplate, as may be the case regarding *El Deafo*. Another example of this is Gene Yang's use of an intentionally ridiculous stereotype in his graphic novel *American Born Chinese*. The character Chin-Kee is a self-conscious, historically informed, stereotypical, and negative representation of the Chinese people meant to be ridiculous in contrast with the *more* realistic and physically differentiated representation of Asian characters in the novel. Chin-Kee is what the main character fears people see him as, so it is an important depiction of a crisis of identity in the novel. Chin-Kee is so over-the-top visually that the rhetorical gesture seems to be that we aren't to see him as an individual, and this is Yang's point. We don't laugh at Chin-Kee from a position of racial superiority but from a position of superiority regarding racist depictions. He is cast in a frame meant to imply a television screen depicting a situation comedy, complete with laugh track. We laugh at the notion that this could be taken seriously, that it is by Jin, and we can do that because of the juxtaposition of cartoon of different degrees of representationalism.

Another example of cartoon used as an effective distancing tool regarding social difference can be found in Michael Willhoite's *Daddy's Roommate*, a 1990 picture book narrated by a young boy whose father has amicably divorced his mother and moved in with another man. When we consider the 1990 publication date, it becomes clear that the book's rhetorical goals are to make the idea of two gay men living together as safe, normal, and nonthreatening to the reader as possible. Part of that strategy is to employ a naïve child narrator who has no agenda but to describe life with Daddy and his friend Frank, which includes the depiction of "normal" things like gardening, going to ball games, going to movies, and making dinner. Daddy and Frank live comfortably in a clean and attractive home and are physically fit, young, white men, making their lives both acceptable and aspirational. The use of cartoon is an effective tool to make these points while still offering an out to uncomfortable readers who require an artistic tool for distancing themselves from this life, however normalized otherwise. The author's use of cartoon, then, is a rhetorical gesture to an implied straight, and potentially uncomfortable adult reader previewing the book.

What is important to consider here is the relationship between distancing techniques and the author's rhetorical intent to either protect the young reader from emotional difficulty or the intent to create a circumstance in which readers are invited to laugh at those different from themselves. We can see both intentions at work in the depiction of diverse characters. The reader should balance what the rhetorical intent seems to be with how the book seems projected to implied readers who are either insiders or outsiders. For instance, I find the cartoon book covers depicting the girls in *One Crazy Summer* counterproductive to the author's rhetorical offering to readers both racially and historically removed from those characters' experiences. The protagonist, Delphine, an African American child who lives in Brooklyn in 1968, is naïve about both her father's and grandmother's experiences with police in Alabama and about the work of the Black Panthers in Oakland. She is our eyes for learning about how her racial community has different ideas about how to cope with oppression, then and now. Big Ma, Delphine's grandmother, believes one should be quiet and not make trouble. Cecile, Delphine's mother, believes in the Black Panthers' approach to protest and demonstration. The reader is meant to sympathize or even empathize with Delphine, our focalizing character, as she and we learn more about racism that she has seemed largely insulated from in her Brooklyn community. The cover art does not provide an effective rhetorical relationship to Delphine and her sisters—we are meant to expect comedy, and it initially distances us from Delphine when we need to build sympathy as soon as possible.

I made the case in chapter 1 that it matters from which direction a character is developed as it moves between the real and unreal. It matters whether the character is becoming more or less recognizable as sympathetic human beings in its journey. It is also the case that it isn't simply a matter of whether a character is smaller than life or lifelike but in what direction it is moving betwixt and between.

There is a sort of developmental gravity that will pull a character from the two different directions of the smaller than life or the larger than life to the life sized—the impulse to increase empathy over time. Some of that is the author's doing—a desire to give a character a soul, so to speak—and some the reader's doing, a desire to grant a character long appreciated over many books a degree of substance by virtue of the weight of familiarity. An aggregate of exposures, of moments, of actions, creates layers in a reading experience, after all. Any number of book series come to mind here: Judy Moody, Junie B. Jones, Ivy & Bean, Encyclopedia Brown, the Boxcar Children, and the Hardy Boys and Nancy Drew mysteries all expose child readers to the same character over and over again in different contexts, necessarily inviting readers to grant the characters history, depth, and intimacy. There is perhaps an unavoidable critical mass regarding character that is achieved over time that authors can't avoid—the more we see the character over a series and over the pages of a particular book, the more round, dynamic, nuanced, historical the character becomes . . . or *seems*. The character and his or her books become associated with our life over time, and we can project our own life experiences onto the character. We remember that when we read that first book, our family took a driving vacation; when we read that next book, there was that difficulty with grandma; when we read another book, we had our first fight with our best friend. So, the change may be as much in ourselves as it is in the character much less in the author's design. This is different but not entirely separate from the ways readers see more in characters through repeated rereadings of a single book. Character realism and reader sympathy created through multiple exposures isn't something an author has complete control over as a communicative act, though in contrast to the phenomenon of a child rereading the same book, an author's continued offering of an otherwise unchanging character can be seen as communicating static consistency yet, ironically, increased intimacy and sympathy.

Moving toward Sympathy

While there are those characters that attain realness or sympathy through an aggregate of exposures, there are those characters in clear transit—in a single book or over a series—from the distance of exaggeration or reduction to the intimacy and sympathy of being life sized. This is accomplished in a number of ways, but always through juxtaposition with other characters that provide a comparative assessment.

The use of narration is one way that authors modulate the rhetorical effect of character, and in the case of modulation from reduced or absurd characters toward sympathy, the power of the storyteller to revise our notions of character is important. A well-known example of an external narrator's modulation or "correction" of character occurs in C. S. Lewis' *The Lion, the Witch and the Wardrobe*. As early as the second page of the narrative, Edmund's boorish behavior is excused by the narrator by saying Edmund was "tired and pretending not to be tired, which always made him bad-tempered" (2). Edmund proceeds to be "beastly" to Lucy through the first part of the book. As Edmund prepares to betray his family to the White Witch, the narrator modulates his character with these words: "You mustn't think that even now Edmund was quite so bad that he actually wanted his brother and sisters to be turned to stone" (96). We are told that Edmund wants to be special for a change, and it is meant to foster pity for him—a first step toward sympathy and empathy. We are told that deep down he knows the White Witch is bad but that he's rationalizing. Edmund is reported to feel sympathy for a group of animals turned to stone (128) as a sort of awakening of an empathetic state of mind, and an invitation is given to us to begin to forgive him the bad choices he has so quickly come to regret. Again, his words and actions have been unforgiving; it is only external narration that modulates him. He acquits himself well in battle at the end of the tale and, when healed of his wounds, "had become his real, old self again and could look you in the face" (197) and has become life sized. Real through external narration. We have the sense that Edmund had become a little so-and-so over time and finally had returned to himself.

While Lewis uses external narration throughout to modify unsympathetic behavior, Frances Hodgson Burnett uses narration to establish an unsympathetic character only to revise it later. *The Secret Garden* employs external narration to establish the actual protagonist Mary Lennox as unsympathetic, pitiful, and smaller than life, an unusual move in a children's book, actually. We are told that "by the time [Mary] was six years old she was a tyrannical and selfish a little pig as ever lived" (10). This is a very subjective and judgmental assessment of her character by the external narrator. Mary "was not an affectionate child and had never cared much for anyone," we are told, and we have no reason to doubt the veracity of our storyteller (13). She is an "ugly, cross little thing" (14). Her behavior isn't just subjectively summarized as "ugly" or "cross" but shown to be so through narrated action and dialogue as we saw with Edmund, though it isn't countered by the narrator at first. As orphaned "Mistress Mary Quite Contrary" (41) has to make her way among the servants and family at Misselthwaite Manor, the narrator begins to ask the reader's consideration for Mary's unusual circumstances: "Even a disagreeable little girl may be lonely," after all (41). As the English countryside "cures" her of her sallowness of body, and exposure to good, white, English people (and not servants in India) transforms her into someone sympathetic to others, the reader grows to sympathize with her as well. As she grows life sized, she encounters Colin, the manor's master's son, who is as disagreeable as she once was. She is capable of feeling sorry for Colin, and strokes the sick boy's hand (138)—much as Edmund develops empathy late in Lewis's novel. Her "hard little heart" grows "quite warm" as she encounters more of the pleasant nature of her new home (168). She is seen to become "downright pretty since she's filled out and lost her ugly little sour look" (249). Mary is modulated through external narration and the comments of other characters to become both sympathetic to the reader and capable of sympathy for another disagreeable character, asking the reader to hope for the modulation of Colin as well. Mary is modulated as a model for what is possible for the master's son—arguably a more important character in the book's universe. Mary becomes the doting girl the 1911 publication date of the novel would have her be.[10]

Authors can use their power to manipulate the reader through the direct, unassailable claims of authority that direct address through external narration has always provided, but authors can also use character narration in subtle ways to achieve the same ends—modulating character from the reduced or exaggerated toward sympathy. A character who believes him- or herself to be one thing (often because of buying into the narrative provided for them by parents, teachers, friends, and siblings) *can* revise their own self-image just as external narration can provide revision from without. It's a matter of choosing one of two powerful forms of authority: the authorial, objective, unassailable voice of external narration or the sympathetic, seductive, and close relationship provided through character narration. *Joey Pigza Swallowed the Key*, a 1998 National Book Award finalist and the first book of the series, shows us a great example of an author building a character from the ridiculous to the sympathetic by having us be persuaded along with the character that he is life sized and worthy of empathy. From the beginning of his own story, Joey tells us that "at school they say I'm wired bad, or wired mad, or wired sad, or wired glad, depending on my mood and what teacher has ended up with me. But there is no doubt about it, I'm *wired*" (3). Joey has severe ADHD and is always getting into trouble. He lives with his grandmother, who tells him, "You don't know what you're doing. You're ruining everything. You never listen to me. I always said you were as dumb as dirt" (14). He then lives with his mother, who means well but provides irregular medication and has Joey believe that it's all and only about choices. His file is full of bad behavior reports. "Hearing stuff like that about me makes me sad," Joey tells his mother (18). "Well, it should," she replies (18). Joey internalizes the narrative about his badness. Mrs. Maxy, his teacher, tells him that he's "losing it" (20) and simply reminds him of the rules regarding sitting still and being quiet. He notes that people always share knowing looks regarding his behavior, and it reaffirms his belief about his worth. He's always being told some version of "stick to the rules and you won't get in trouble" (40); Joey is made to see that his behavior is related only to willful disobedience, and we follow Joey's own thinking on this as he narrates. At the book's end, Joey is told by the parent of a classmate that "the medication has helped settle you down, but you have been a good kid all along. You are naturally good. I hope you know that about yourself. You have a good heart" (153). This is a revelation to Joey, and to the young reader perhaps as well. Joey is touched by this, as is the reader. The reader might have liked Joey all along, but seeing Joey's actions through Joey's own interpretation tinged by the reported speech of his mother, grandmother, and teacher offer, it's easy to also buy into Joey's badness. Joey as a character becomes more sympathetic as he, the narrator, sees himself having value, making it more possible—creating an invitation—for the young reader to see it, too. Arguably the older, more mature reader feels sympathy all along. The writer asks the young reader to revise her notion of the character, moving from pathetic to sympathetic while simultaneously recognizing that the character was inherently sympathetic all along. It was perception of character that was modulated rather than character.

Some characters are modulated toward sympathetic, life-sized status by constant exposure instead of active revision; some characters are modulated by information received from the external narrator; some are offer modulated perception rather than actuality through character narration. One more technique involves modulating character through the readers' (and author's awareness of readers') existing knowledge of a simplified version of that character. The novelization of folktales for young readers takes smaller-than-life characters and makes them life sized. We can point to any number of examples of this, including such successful novelizations as Robin McKinley's *Beauty* and Gail Carson Levine's *Ella Enchanted*. These authors' implied reader is the one knowledgeable of the characters in folktale form; the rhetorical manipulation of character takes the pre-existing interest and even basic sympathy and builds a complicated (but not contradictory) version of that smaller-than-life model. In these cases, readers are only asked to consider the characters in more sympathetic detail rather than revising any conclusions about them. A form of this is the recasting of emphasis on a particular character, as found in Gregory Maguire's retellings of Cinderella (*Confessions of an Ugly Stepsister*) and *The Wonderful Wizard of Oz* (*Wicked*). Secondary characters are made more sympathetic through a revision of motives, the shift in character narration for belief and authority, and success in getting the reader to doubt the veracity of the former tale. The "real" story pushes characters who are absurd toward sympathetic realness.[9]

Character sympathy can be modulated by means of other characters. Two classic children's books ask us to have sympathy for characters because of the work—and ultimate disappearance—of other characters. This is a rhetorical tactic that not only increases the sympathy for an otherwise unremarkable character but also presents the reader with two different modalities through those characters' respective stories. Mode came to my attention for another reason, however. It was only after successive class discussions about *Charlotte's Web*, *Bridge to Terabithia*, and *Tuck Everlasting* that I realized that a particular use of mode helps modulate character and might even be one explanation for the success of certain "classic" books that I also consider "crossover books," or books that appeal to both children and adults. Students who had read these books years before and who had reread them for my class found that their responses had changed over time, though those responses were still positive. Something was different for those readers, however. I had planned to focus on genre difference: *Charlotte's Web* is an animal fantasy, *Bridge to Terabithia* is contemporary/New Realism, and *Tuck Everlasting* is mixed fantasy/historical fiction. Those differences didn't seem to matter to my students very much, though. How those books presented two modes/characters and what it meant for developing the sympathy for character was more interesting to them.

One book that gives both children and adults pleasure is *Charlotte's Web*. In their guest editors' introduction to a special issue of the journal *Children's Literature* on cross-writing, U. C. Knoepflmacher and Mitzi Myers present two students who report a change in the pleasure they have derived from *Charlotte's Web* over the years.[9] One student reports a shift in her relationship to character: while as a child she "joyfully identified" with Wilbur (ix), as a twenty-year-old she is touched by Charlotte's sacrifice and her ability to accept the inevitable (x). For both students, Wilbur becomes "diminished," while Charlotte's status is elevated (x). My students found this to be true as well. Frye observes that since antiquity, it has been character that distinguishes one literary work from another, not genre (33). Mode is a character-driven theory at its heart, after all, for it focuses on defining the nature of the protagonist through her fate, and it best accounts for the shift in both our attention in and understanding of this book as we grow more experienced and mature.

Charlotte's Web is an animal fantasy. What impresses the young readers, however, is Wilbur's comedy; what matters more to their elders is Charlotte's tragedy.[11] "Pig" and "spider" matter much less. I recall an observation by one of my professors in an undergraduate class as we read *King Lear*, an observation that he claimed was shared with him by one of his professors years before: we sympathize with Cordelia when we are young adults; Lear becomes the sympathetic character to us if we later have children of our own. This appeal by age and experience is comparable to what we find in *Charlotte's Web*. Norton Kinghorn notes that critics have been mixed on not only what the novel "is about," but about which character "there is even less agreement" (4). Rebecca Lukens claims in her 1976 edition of *A Critical Handbook of Children's Literature* that Wilbur is the protagonist (Kinghorn 4), and John Griffith portrays Charlotte as "the best antidote to [Wilbur's] boredom" (115). The novel is about both, of course, but they aren't starring in the same story—or, more to the point, they aren't experiencing and presenting the same modes, and perhaps because of that, one character is the protagonist in a story for children, the other in a story for adults. In any case, two appeals to emotion are made by the end of the book, and one character's story and role will modulate the other character toward a more sympathetic reception by the reader.

Wilbur's is the story of comedy as it approaches the ironic, for he is a pig rich in unearned luck. Wilbur is much less sympathetic in the beginning than many a droll character who succeeds through luck rather than through cleverness, bravery, or moral goodness. His success comes in spite of his character, not because of it. Readers will find his self-absorption pitiable, though funny (in direct contrast to Templeton's loathsome solipsism), and we want him to survive to whine and dine another day. I ask those in my class who claim to have read the book before as children what they remember about the plot. Surprisingly, few of my students remember the details of Charlotte's fate. Her fate might be forgotten as we focus on Wilbur's triumphant return, or perhaps we are entirely ignorant of Charlotte's death because a well-meaning, censorial adult read to us.[12] Charlotte's is the story of tragedy as it approaches the romantic. She is what Frye calls a high mimetic character—one who is superior to other characters by degree but not, ultimately, superior to her environment (usually reserved to the gods of myth).[13] Self-conscious sacrifice rather than irony marks her death. Her "flaw" is not pride but nature. While she is fated to die much sooner than Wilbur, she doesn't bemoan using her small span of time helping Wilbur. While the ignoble Wilbur is "spared horrific death," which

Frye notes is true of many ironic comedies (175), and returns home to root, Charlotte dies with dignity and a sense of dual accomplishment (saving Wilbur and laying her eggs) apart from the society of the barn for as is true for tragic heroes, the improved world is not for them. Frye notes the tendency in fiction to either integrate the hero with society (comedy) or to isolate that character (tragedy) (54); this is certainly the case in *Charlotte's Web*. Tragedy and comedy "contrast rather than blend," Frye tells us, "and so do romance and irony" (162). Charlotte's more romantic tragedy contrasts with the ironic comedy starring Wilbur. The modes do not blend; they are entwined. They appeal to different people in differing degrees, to what we are and were and will become over time, to our mood and turn of mind from moment to moment. This isn't necessarily a matter of age, but it can be.

What we see, too, is that Wilbur is modulated from the ridiculous to a more real and sympathetic position in his care of Charlotte's eggs and subsequent children, grandchildren, and beyond. After Charlotte's death, Wilbur becomes grateful, helpful, and responsible. White modulates Charlotte for the child reader, if not also the adult reader, to be worthy of sympathy; before, he was only pitiable and small. He is at the end what Charlotte wrote of him, made him: Some Pig. Importantly, though, each character is used to push the other toward a more sympathetic reading by the child. What starts as selfish pig and dabbling spider ends with both characters ennobled—one through death and the other through obligation to the others' progeny.

The genre under which *Bridge to Terabithia* is discussed in handbooks is "realism." That's why it was on my syllabus. Its role as an example of New Realism often overshadows its other qualities. A colleague of mine once referred to it as "that book about death for children"—no doubt others have so reduced it. I wanted to see how students responded to death as a subject in a different genre for children after they had read *Charlotte's Web*. I wanted to see whether their response to the portrayal and presence of death would be different if the characters were human. It turns out that the difference in genre was not terribly important to them, though it remains true that the anthropomorphism of Charlotte distances us from her death if only a little. Here was another book with two distinct and opposing modes. In fact, my students were intent on making the Leslie-Charlotte and Jess-Wilbur parallels by gender, role, implied differences in maturity (if not age), and fate. And I had to assure them with some embarrassment that I hadn't seen the parallel, much less used that as my rationale for placing them side-by-side on the syllabus.

Like *Charlotte's Web*, *Bridge to Terabithia* offers us tragedy and comedy through a pair of protagonists, one of whom, a young boy, is helped by someone more mature and wiser, who will die by the book's end. This is not to say, as my students suggest, that Charlotte is an eight-legged Leslie, and Jess is a slightly less dirty version of Wilbur. Jess and Leslie's relationship is more complicated and deals with the subtexts of gender, guilt, and family in ways White's book does not. Jess's story, though comedic by mode, leans more toward romance than the irony found in Wilbur's tale. Jess is sexist, selfish, and jealous early on in his treatment of Maybelle, his little sister, and Leslie, the new girl who is faster than any boy in their class. He is small-minded. Following his loss of Leslie, Jess becomes more generous and open-minded, as seen in his inclusion of Maybelle in Terabithia at book's end. He has grown a bit closer to his father through grief, though it's hard to say whether that was a momentary closeness or the beginning of something more substantial. Maria Nikolajeva observes about the story that "we may be thoroughly upset by Leslie's death, but for Jess it provides a substantial thrust toward spiritual maturity. In fact, the ending shows him at least partially recuperated and definitely strong enough to go further" (174).[14]

In *Charlotte's Web*, the focus might be on either of the characters depending on the reader's mood, age, maturity, or personal inclination—how they respond to the rhetorical offering of the author. Both characters are pushed from the absurd to life-sized sympathy. *Bridge to Terabithia* is Jess's story, ultimately. Wilbur, though not the title character, remains an option for focus because his ironic life is comedic rather than tragic; but since Leslie's tragedy is marked by irony, we have little choice but to conclude that Jess is the right focus for our attention in what remains a children's book. And while

Charlotte dies as an "adult," Leslie's death combines the senselessness of irony with the loss of a child. "Dying in season evokes no terrors," John Griffith argues about *Charlotte's Web*, and there Charlotte's dying in season is combined with her "immortality" as a mother, her noble sacrifice of her remaining time, and her being tired and ready for death. Arguably, while the complementary modes of tragedy and irony can be tempered by their respective complementary modes of romance and comedy, the mixture of tragedy and irony puts us in a much more traditionally adult context. Unless the tragic-ironic is seen as acceptable as a rhetorical relationship with a perceived child reader, and it isn't, this is Jess's story. For it to be Leslie's story is for the irony of senseless loss to be the focus, after all—for unjust randomness to rule. Leslie is not unlike Charlotte as high mimetic character, but she is ironic in her fate. Northrop Frye's description of the tragic irony fits Leslie's condition:

> The central principle of tragic irony is that whatever exceptional happens to the hero should be causally out of line with his character. . . . Tragedy is intelligible because its catastrophe is plausibly related to its situation. Irony isolates from the tragic situation the sense of arbitrariness, of the victim's having been unlucky, selected at random or by lot. . . . If there is a reason for choosing him for catastrophe, it is an inadequate reason, and raises more objections than it answers. (41)

Leslie, like Charlotte, leaves her charge behind to fend for himself; unlike Charlotte's death, however, Leslie's is not sacrifice. It is Jess's response to Leslie's life and death that will create meaning and make him a sympathetic rather than small-minded boy. Wilbur's comedic and ironic response cannot change the grandeur of Charlotte's knowing sacrifice. Jess can make Leslie meaningless in this story simply by doing what Wilbur does: return to life exactly as it was before. Frank Kermode writes of the end of the tragic tale that "the world goes forward in the hands of exhausted survivors" (82). The exhaustion is greater following the ironic death, arguably, because of our inability to adequately prepare for it—either as readers or as "characters" caught in a tragic-ironic plot. Joel Chaston makes an important point when he tells us that though Jess and Leslie encounter death in stories throughout the novel, "the stories that they encounter do not, however, treat purposeless, accidental death, the kind that comes when least expected" (239), which might argue that Paterson herself doesn't want us to dwell on the ironic.[15] For the world to go forward, the reader must focus on Jess and Wilbur—characters who have become real to us and worthy of sympathy and, perhaps, empathy.

Both of these classic novels are surprising in their plots, which is itself surprising. All stories are about their endings, after all—or, perhaps, all endings make their stories about something—and the use of peripeteia, or the surprising shift of plot, is least employed in myth, folklore, and children's fiction—forms that traditionally follow fairly clear narrative trajectories. "The story that proceeded very simply to its obviously predestined end would be nearer myth than novel or drama," and therefore life as well (Kermode 18). It is the combination of modes that creates this partial and surprising peripeteia in the two novels. I say "partial" because the stories of Jesse and Wilbur end in ways both expected and hoped for by design—the characters are safe and either have grown or simply prosper. We want and hope, though, that Charlotte and Leslie will be with their co-protagonists to enjoy it.[16] The fact that we are simultaneously given and denied what we want makes the stories richer, more complex, and more interesting for that paradox. If the child dwells on the wish fulfilled and misses or ignores the more complex larger view, it will be there when she is ready, as her parents are ready.

These novels cross over by mode and, as I've been implying, by audience. Peter Neumeyer argues that E. B. White is "archly addressing the parents over the heads of children," which, he claims, is tantamount to the author "breaking faith" with his audience (74). But I don't think the book ultimately divides readers. Attentive children with life experience can be touched by Charlotte's sacrifice even as they cheer Wilbur's salvation; and adults are no less happy for the droll pig even while they might dwell on the beauty of the selfless acts that led to that salvation. I think this book as well as Paterson's achieves Wall's "dual-audience" designation, wherein a book appeals to both children and adults simultaneously rather than in an alternating and distracting way, which she calls "double address." These authors are no Milnes or Barries winking over the heads of children to the adults lined up in the back of the room. Instead, they offer audiences of all ages contrasting and simultaneous modes. Rather than a breach of faith, the offering is the ultimate act of faith in both young readers' abilities and adults' willingness to expose children to the special beauty of tragedy.

This clever use of simultaneous modes is one reason for both a book's successful crossing over and its longevity. People have long noted that a book that doesn't appeal to parents won't last long. Children's books that successfully entwine contrasting modes ensure that there is an emotional offering that will be available to any reader, despite age, and depending on his or her mood or need. In fact, it's more likely that we can actually experience the balancing effects of both contrasting emotions: I can smile at Wilbur as a remaining tear shed for Charlotte runs down my cheek; as I still feel the stunning effects of Leslie's loss, I can smile at Jess's gesture to allow Maybelle into Terabithia. Crossing by mode, entwining by mode, gives us an emotional both/and, and whatever the age, disposition, or inclination, there will be an effect on the reader. Rather than being torn in two directions, as we are when we read double-addressed books that have inside jokes for adults mixed in with appeals to the interests of children, we are allowed to be our most complex human selves by experiencing contrasting emotions simultaneously. These modal contrasts don't point us in two different directions; they give us two different feelings that balance each other—the lighter modes are given more weight, and the weightier modes are put into perspective. They are rhetorically sophisticated. The use of simultaneous modes in a book that is marketed for children sets that young reader up for several possible reading experiences. The book ensures that readers differently able to understand or access different modal expressions of the world will be rewarded, and built into the book's design is a transitional experience for those less able or likely to recognize all that is present. Such a book provides for the reader able to recognize and understand both modes the pleasure of juxtaposition: here is the world in its complex glory. Such a book provides the ready reader the big picture that, like the world itself, doesn't demand that the reader dwell on all of its complexity at once. A book for children that entwines modes with characters that modulate each other will reward successive readings, which is a quality that we tend to value. These books will match or challenge whatever mood or frame of mind with which we arrive. There are the books that are of no use to us once we know the ending, but those that entwine contrasting modes make the ending richer and less "knowable," even if they are "closed" endings. Such books give us new ways to consider what constitutes a successful "crossover." Publishers and bookstores tend to divide children's and adult books by mode, though less than they used to, doling out the droll to the child and keeping him or her "safe" from irony and tragedy. White and Paterson show us that there are both opportunities to and rewards for authors who ignore such simple divisions.

Moving toward Pity

While there is an equal and compelling reason for authors to pull characters in either direction from life-sized/like toward the larger-than-life characters (trading *awwww* for awe, or the reverse)—there are fewer compelling reasons for authors to modulate characters toward the simplified or exaggerated from the life sized. Under what circumstances might an author want to simplify or exaggerate an already realistic, sympathetic character? It's one thing to create a character that is static and smaller than life, but to push it there from empathy seems an odd choice. Like the move from the life sized to larger than life, it trails clouds of empathy from whence it came, but when is it rhetorically advantageous to do that? Modulation from the sympathetic to the smaller than life retains humanity in the face of the increasingly ridiculous. It's sad. It's potentially unsettling. Any modulation toward the ridiculous diffuses/de-fuses character. Unlike the move from real to larger than life, which can have the compensatory effect of grandeur for the loss of identification, the move from the real to the exaggerated is only a loss of humanity. It's necessarily a diminishment. It asks of the reader to see less humanity in a character, and it's a sort of defeat for the character, and perhaps the author in his or her inability to sustain interest in the emotional connection to a character.

The characters about which my students have expressed an unease share the quality of trying to be both sympathetic and exaggerated. One in particular is unusual because the absurdity and exaggeration that feels laughable is meant, I think, to evoke pathos in the reader. Kristina in Ellen Hopkins' *Crank* and subsequent books is this sort of character. It is the character from the cautionary tale, and the cautionary tale has not been in vogue in literature for the young for a long time. There is, especially in the beginning of the first *Crank* novel, a reality to the character. She is plausible and identifiable as a young girl who wants to visit and get to know her father. The development of her alter ego is, by the end of the first book, almost fantastic in its depiction. The shifting of the verse forms with each entry over hundreds of pages has already had the effect of distraction for the reader, but Kristina has become not just warped as a person due to her addiction to meth, but her depiction by Hopkins feels more like a combination of *The Exorcist* and *Sybil*.[17]

It's important to point out that these are all YA novels rather than children's novels, which may suggest that these authors believe their readers to be able to make sense of the movement from the real to the exaggerated. It's harder to think of such communicated unease with younger readers—characters tend to be more clearly real or exaggerated in those contexts and decidedly more likely to move from one to the other through modulation by authors. So, this particular direction on the dial of rhetorical modulation—from life sized to smaller than life—is clearly a YA convention and not something authors typically offer to young children. It could be that authors writing for young children unconsciously know that this direction demands a sense of pity or loss or disappointment that only older readers can experience without condemning this depiction of humanity as "wrong" or "against the rules" of the triumph even of tragedy. An ironic development and a modulation of character are not offered up to children.[18]

In chapter 1, I argued against the notion of character "growth" in favor of the idea of "change." The author changes what a character means, through revelation of information, back story, epiphany, and any number of rhetorical narrative moves. I raise this point here because I want to argue equally against the idea of the fallen character. Literary characters don't have dark nights of the soul that cause them to become lesser, absurd, or pathetic creatures; authors decide that they want to communicate different things to the reader through character. Jerry Renault in Robert Cormier's *The Chocolate War* is a character in decline, the main character in a YA cautionary tale. Cormier clearly communicates some things through Jerry. It is important for Jerry to be modulated throughout the novel in order for us to find him useful as a caution. Cormier begins the novel with a highly sympathetic portrait of Jerry as a regular kid trying to make the freshman football team. He tells himself that he has the guts that the coach is looking for, and he shows it, making him begin the novel somewhere between life sized and larger than life, really (8). His toughness earns him a return trip to try-outs. At the end of the first, brief chapter, Jerry seems admirable. Archie, the character who will turn out to be the Byronic villain of the novel, is impressed with Archie's guts (17) and will end up manipulating Jerry's headstrong nature. Archie, a key member of the school's secret society, the Vigils, is in charge of giving younger students "assignments" that mess with the school's authority. He picks Jerry to refuse to sell his share of chocolates for the school fundraiser. It will be Jerry's relationship to this prank that modulates him from admirable all the way to pitiable and smaller than life. It doesn't take much, it turns out.

At first, it is clear to the other students that Jerry is under orders, so they think nothing much of his refusals, though Jerry risks angering the dangerous Brother Leon (68). When Jerry has been told to stand down from refusal by Archie, Jerry chooses to disturb the universe. Midnovel, Jerry refuses when he is supposed to accept, and after his "no" has stopped echoing in the room, "Cities fell. Earth opened. Planets tilted. Stars plummeted. And the awful silence" (88).

This ends chapter 17. The beginning of chapter 18 is key to Jerry's modulation. In the gap between the two chapters, Jerry earns, briefly, a status as conscientious objector—someone not under orders but following his beliefs. He is defying both the Vigils and the school. He dares to disturb the universe. Cormier does a simple thing to begin Jerry's modulation ineluctably toward pity and smallness. "WHY DID YOU DO IT?" Jerry's friend Goober asks (89). "I don't know" is Jerry's answer (89). He never relents, and he never knows why. From here on out in the novel, Jerry is a purely headstrong character. It harkens back to the football opening scene. Coach asks him why he wants to play this game he's beaten up in. Jerry doesn't have an answer. Our admiration turns to something else. Pity. His courage is now simply obstinacy. He's beaten to a pulp at the end of the book, and he thinks to warn Goober "to play ball, to play football, to run, to make the team, to sell the chocolates, to sell whatever they wanted you to sell, to do whatever they wanted you to do" (187). Jerry is broken, and it's his own fault. Anita Tarr argues that "it is just an illusion created by Cormier that Jerry is a rebel against an unjust system" (99), but in arguing against the position that Jerry is a hero, Tarr also doesn't give Cormier credit for consciously making him a cautionary tale. Jerry is modulated by Cormier toward pity, and we are to conclude that Jerry only had it partly right. Disturb the universe, but have a plan. Jerry fails because Archie has a plan, and Jerry doesn't. Courage becomes recklessness.

Another YA novel that modulates a character from sympathy or life sized to pity or smallness is M. T. Anderson's dystopic comedy (yes) *Feed*. Titus's decline from sympathy to pity is absolute. Titus is weak and unready to rise to the occasion, so Anderson's modulation of Titus through the deteriorating health of his girlfriend, Violet, moves him from sympathetic and naïve to pitiable and contemptible. The reader has to forgive Titus his weakness . . . or not. Titus goes from the only kid in his group that uses figurative language, an attraction to home-schooled and bright Violet (63), to being unequipped emotionally to be there for her when she fades. Near the end of novel, Titus tries to excuse his failure to be there for her: "I didn't sign up to go out with you forever when you're dead. It's been a couple of months. Okay? A couple of months," and coupled with some cruel and selfish jibes at her, causes Violet to tell him, "I discover that I hate you" (273). We have to decide ourselves whether we do or simply pity his weakness. Despite his decision to visit her on her deathbed, Titus never recovers sympathy. He remains ridiculous. Small. In both *The Chocolate War* and *Feed*, other characters are used to modulate protagonists toward smallness and to drive the reader toward pity.

I'd like to end with an extended look at another YA title in which the author uses secondary characters as rhetorical tools to modulate the main character toward pity. The difference here is that this book's presentation of the main character as pitiable isn't obvious; in fact, one would think that there is triumph at the end, though the reader would have an uneasy feeling of triumph. Gene Luen Yang's Printz Award–winning graphic novel *American Born Chinese* has been hailed as a hallmark of YA literature dealing with race and ethnicity. Scholars have addressed the book's treatment of racial identity (beyond complaints of racial stereotype); what remains unconsidered is the life that lies ahead of Jin Wang and what the author suggests about Jin's acceptance of his identity—an identity ultimately accepted through the persuasion of a secondary character. While it is true, as one review of the novel characterizes, that the novel is "a well-crafted work that aptly explores issues of self-image, cultural identity, transformation, and self-acceptance" and that "this novel explores the impact of the American dream on those outside the dominant culture" (Crawford 240), it fails to point out exactly what those explorations yield. Jared Gardner points out that Yang's novel doesn't "promise that cultural identity offers a safe haven or an easy answer" and that Yang uses the "graphic narrative's necessarily interactive nature to force the reader into a position of taking an active role in making meaning out of what can't be spoken: the conclusions, the road map as to how to move forward" (147), but my complaint isn't against open-endedness; it's about trajectory. I would agree with Gardner's assertion about the freeing open-endedness that the novel offered if it hadn't the parallel narrative of the Monkey King, a narrative that concludes with a promise of the Monkey

King's perpetual subservience, set up against Jin Wang's narrative. The guard at the door of the party that opens the book makes it clear that the Monkey King "may be a king—[he] may even be a deity—but [he is] still a monkey" (15), so he may not enter the party. The rest of the novel takes on the question of what it *means* to be a monkey . . . or (as the parallel narrative suggests) an American-born Chinese. What does it mean for the reader of any ethnicity to see Jin Wang identify with the Monkey King at the end of the story? I argue that the author uses the character of the Monkey King to drive the protagonist toward smallness despite the book's successful arguments against embracing racial stereotypes.

The story is told in three interwoven narrative strands set up in three different parts. Two strands are directly related by character and time, though they shift in genre; one strand is the book's introductory narrative featuring the story of the Chinese mythological figure of the Monkey King. This narrative tells the story of how the Monkey King is laughed out of heaven upon attempting to enter a party for deities. Though he is himself a deity, he is told that because he is also a monkey, he is not permitted to enter. He rages against the injustice and attacks the guard and all of the deities in attendance. He returns to his home and engages in advanced kung fu in order to make himself not only more powerful but different. He emerges in the shape of a man rather than in the shape of a monkey and terrorizes those who mocked him. The other deities complain to the emissaries of Tze-Yo-Tzuh, the creator of all things, who tries to counsel the Monkey King to accept his identity as a monkey, which he has abandoned. When he refuses, the Monkey King is imprisoned under a mountain of stone for five hundred years until the monk Wong Lai-Tsao shows up to enlist him as a disciple.

The second strand is the story of Jin Wang, a first-generation American-born boy of Chinese ethnicity. He moves from a Chinese community in San Francisco to an unspecified Anglo community in the United States and tries to navigate the complicated ethnic ignorance and prejudice of teachers and fellow students.

The third strand turns out to be an extension of the second: Jin Wang is transformed at the end of his narrative into "Danny," a blue-eyed, fair-haired Anglo adolescent. The story shifts from a principally realistic narrative into a situation comedy (complete with a laugh track) starring a racially and ethnically stereotyped character named "Chin Key," purportedly Danny's cousin, who visits Danny and causes him untold embarrassment.

The three strands are presented in three groups. In the first triad of strands, we see the introduction of the challenge to the respective protagonists' identity; in the second, we see the conscious choice of the main character to change himself to fit better into the culture; in the third, we see the revelation of each character and an acceptance of himself and his place in culture. At the end of the third triad, the Monkey King reveals himself to be Chin Key, Jin Wang's "conscience" and a "sign-post to [Jin Wang's/Danny's] soul" (221), and Jin Wang's estranged friend Wei-Chen is revealed to be the disillusioned son of the Monkey King. The book ends with these three strands coming together and Jin Wang both accepting his identity and reconciling with Wei-Chen.

Recently, Ramón Saldívar has offered the term "speculative realism" as a "way of getting at the revisions of realism and fantasy into speculative forms that are seeming to shape the invention of new narrative modes in contemporary fiction" (3). "Speculative realism [is] a hybrid crossing of the fictional modes of the speculative genres, naturalism, social realism, surrealism, magical realism, 'dirty' realism, and metaphysical realism" (5). Speculative realism is part of Saldívar's "Postrace aesthetic" that explores the thematics of race in the new millennium. "One way in which this speculative realism appears is allegorically, as a basis for recognizing and understanding the construction of the new political destinies we may witness taking shape among diasporic groups in the US today" (14). While Saldívar does not discuss Yang's work, it seems clear that Yang is just such a writer. Yang blends forms (graphic novel and YA literature) with genres (folklore, fantasy, realism) to investigate the implications of race in the twenty-first century. Multiple relationships are investigated in the narrative. The blend of genres enables Yang to consider the relationship between animal, machine, and human, which allows for consideration of the degree to which identity is chosen, constructed, or simply inherited and accepted (essentialism). *American Born Chinese* is an experiment in discussing minority racial identity through metaphor made possible through genre blending. The experiment leaves us ultimately with a parallel between a monkey god from folklore and a YA American-born Chinese in a realistic context. The narratives rotate between fantasy based on the ancient Chinese legends to the *bildungsroman* of a Chinese American boy to an absurd "sit-com" presentation about a stereotypical Chinese attending his white cousin's high school. While Gene Yang himself has discussed the implications of his use of the consciously stereotypical Chin-Key (buck-toothed, speech-impeded, overachieving, lascivious, cat-eating) in his Printz acceptance speech, little attention has been paid to the more subtle issue of racial identity: what does it mean for the Monkey King to be a monkey, a content and subservient monkey, and what does it mean for him to suggest that Jin accept what is implied to be a parallel position? Much of what that means is determined in this genre blending because we are left with a direct comparison between the principle figure of the mythological tale and the principle figure of the *bildungsroman* in realism.

Children's literature often employs animal characters as a way to distance the reader from the demographics of character, as I have discussed previously. All characters might be mice or badgers for no reason, in contrast to the metaphoric use of animals in folklore that serve as shorthand for virtue and vice. Race is often removed from a narrative with the use of animals, though certainly it can be present through the use of historically and culturally endorsed symbols of race, such as the Monkey (See Song's essay for more history on this particular use). In this YA graphic novel, the animal character is placed next to the human coprotagonist as a way to provide a parallel narrative of epiphany regarding essential racial identity and its attendant role in society. We might consider the animal as used in this specifically YA narrative. The animal character stands in for ambiguity, the transitional, the belittled, the *adolescent*—as in the case of the eponymous Stuart Little (Gubar). John Morganstern contends that it all depends on the angle from which you look at the animal character—is it an animal-man or man-animal? Is it an adolescent becoming adult or the mark of insufficient development of the species or race?

The animal character in this novel ends up serving as metaphor about race, whatever else it might do. It isn't an innocent stand-in as in much children's literature; it has a history of racist associations; it is used as a marker of transition to the adult and self-acceptance of identity, a genre-defining theme in YA literature. The reader is left to infer how the conclusions the Monkey King comes to about his identity and role in the cosmos are applicable to Jin Wang as an American-born Chinese. Very early in the novel's first narrative strand, the Monkey King takes on human shape after his humiliation at being rejected from the party in heaven. His new shape not only is a rejection of his monkey nature but also is the shape of true power and worth in this narrative world. Tze-Yo-Tzuh is human in appearance, after all. Tze-Yo-Tzuh finds the Monkey King's new shape a problem, saying, "I created you. I say that you are a monkey, therefore you are a monkey" (69) and then a few pages later, "A monkey I intended you to be. A monkey you are" (81). The Monkey King decides to take his "true" form when he finally subjects himself to Tze-Yo-Tzuh's will. In all cases—the Monkey King's, his son's, Jin Wang's—the initial transformation is from not merely one form to another, but from what is perceived to be the lesser form to the greater. To move from monkey to human (even if one is also a deity) is a move "up" in terms of creation; a move from Chinese American to European American is also a step up in another hierarchy—racial dominance. The Monkey King has to relinquish this superior shape he has assumed. Jin becomes Danny, the white boy, in the third narrative—either literally or psychologically—until he is turned back by the Monkey King. I say "turned back," though it might be more fitting to say "released," as it is a release of kung fu that returns the Monkey King to his "true" shape. Jin Wang is fighting physical and/or psychological nature to maintain his Danny form. When the Monkey King sheds his Chin-Key disguise and reveals himself to Danny, he tells him, "Now that I've revealed my **true form**, perhaps it is time to reveal **yours . . . Jin Wang**" (213–14). "True form" is in bold in the text. This is an intervention implied to be for Jin's own good as well as the good of the order of things. He is reshaped, released, returned. He is put back into his place by one who has been put into his own place, which suggests the internalization of that inferiority by one oppressed.

A second metaphor for identity that the novel features to complement the essentialist animal/racial metaphor is one of mechanism, and this is principally told in the section of the narrative devoted to realism. One would assume that such a metaphor would balance social construction with essentialism in order to complicate the issue as the "speculative realistic" text ought. The novel introduces early on a metaphor for transforming oneself. Jin plays with a Transformer action figure—a metaphor that we are directly invited to consider by the narrative. The toy can change from a robot to a truck and back again. Jin tells an old woman who asks him what he wants to be when he grows up that he wants to be a Transformer. He explains it as being "more than meets the eye" (28). Here it seems like he is expressing the desire to be mysterious, versatile, adaptable, complex, undetermined, and what the situation calls for—something that the narrative value system of the novel never again raises as a legitimate option. The old woman dramatically warns him, "It's easy to become anything you wish . . . so long as you're willing to forfeit your soul" (29). The metaphor of mechanism has an essentialist reading imposed on it here. The Transformer is given a soul and a primary setting. The old woman's statement is followed by awkward silence depicted through dialogue and narration-free illustration so that this information can sink in. The reader is left with the powerful suggestion that to change is really to sell oneself out (and potentially others). The Transformer toy becomes a metaphor for deception—either of lying to oneself about what one is or as a tool to deceive others for a (good) purpose. When the Monkey King sends his own son to help Jin, he gives the young, transformed monkey a Transformer toy that moves between the forms of monkey and robot. "Let [the Transformer] remind you of who you are," the Monkey King advises his son (217). How should the Transformer serve to remind him? How does the Transformer serve as a metaphor? When a toy can assume two forms, which one of them is the "true" form?

Does a Transformer, something that can be either thing, present the possibility of a "wrong" form? The novel itself is pretty clear about transformation—it should be temporary and only used to serve others. One has an essential identity, and one should return to it.

In *American Born Chinese*, intentional transformation for change is never a real option. It is self-delusion. It's clear either way that it's wrong for Jin to choose to be Danny—for him to make a change or even to desire it, so the degree to which this narrative is open-ended is questionable. The Monkey King tells Jin that he comes to serve as Jin's "conscience—as a sign post to [Jin's] soul" (221). When Jin asks the Monkey King, "So what am I supposed to do now?" (223), he is told, "You know, Jin, I would have saved myself from five hundred years' imprisonment beneath a mountain of rock had I only realized how good it is to be a monkey" (223). It is here that we, and Jin, are given the only answer that the novel provides to that question, but that answer is pretty clear. The Monkey King tells how he should have realized how good it is to be a monkey, but he's never really "just" a monkey: he's an anthropomorphized deity. He's been told by his creator, however, that a *monkey* is what he is. Regardless of what else he is, and how impressive those sites of identity are, "Monkey" is the primary setting. He may be a king, he may even be a deity, but he is primarily and essentially and *only* a monkey.

Yang's narrative performs a tricky but subtle evasion following the final interchange between the Monkey King and Jin. The explicit essentialist claim made by the ironically anthropomorphized character is offered in juxtaposition to Jin's situation. After all, the novel invites us to focus on the parallels between the Monkey King's experience and Jin Wang's. Both tales are *bildungsromane* that conclude with the presumed reincorporation of the rebellious youth into society "as himself" but with self-awareness and maturity. This is a YA novel, after all. Each character begins content with his lot in life, ignorant of the race/species bias of others in the world. Each has his own revelation that his would-be peers consider him inferior. Each character responds with anger and self-loathing that implies an acceptance of that inferiority. They each reconstitute themselves through a transformation that leads to destructive behavior, and each is encouraged to resume his original and "true" form by a deity—that is, after being convinced by that deity what the true and only possibility is. In Jin's case, the persuasive deity is the Monkey King himself. Their respective stories conclude with the persuaded character accepting his "real" and divinely intended self, which is in an inferior position relative to others of his kind.

The Monkey King offers his narrative as a parallel to Jin's: "It's good to be a monkey." So what is the equivalent of "monkey" for Jin? What is Jin Wang's essential defining feature? Not his humanity, his gender, his age, or some unique and special quality. No. Jin Wang is first and last a racial minority in the way that the Monkey King is first and last a monkey. It's good to be a racial minority. To accept that apparently means to be subordinate, to listen to popular, white Greg who, like Tze-Yo-Tzu, can put the lesser one of his kind in his place. Our "betters" have the power (and responsibility) to make us recognize ourselves as what they say we are . . . as inferior to the main group and, well, still not invited to the party. Their being "better" depends upon it, after all. We buy it. It is sold down the chain from Tze-Yo-Tzu to the Monkey King, from the Monkey King to Jin Wang, from Jin Wang to Wei-Chen. We could argue that the Monkey King sells to Jin what might be considered the path of least resistance, though that isn't the argument made for acceptance. The book does not end with the Monkey at the party or Jin at the prom (or anywhere) with Amelia. The narratives end with the great Monkey King a servant to humanity and Jin Wang self-segregated from the larger community. As Tze-Yo-Tzuh tells the recalcitrant Monkey King that he is a "silly little monkey" (69) among more important deities, Jin is left a "silly little Chinese" among more important ethnicities at the end of the narrative—implicitly inferior in status to his white counterparts, though presumably as content and at as much peace as the Monkey King in his "true form."

This is not really a choice; it's about domestication, and it is the will of heaven, no less. Yang's parallel narrative infuses the Jin Wang narrative with a sense of heavenly destiny. Don't fight it. It's the way of the universe. Not only is it a losing fight, but it's also wrong to fight it. Lan Dong tells us that "such an ending indicates the hope that the characters may finally make peace with their true identities" (245), and Hathaway argues that the Monkey King urges Jin to reconcile with his own identity and with Wei-Chen (47). What they don't tell us is what such "peace" and "reconciliation" mean. Min Hyoung Song invites us to examine the relationship between the racialized monkey image and Wei-Chen that "points directly to the need to confront a painful visual history of racial disparagement that has equated the animal with the subhuman" (92). That confrontation is necessary, but it isn't invited by Yang's narrative. Yang's narrative shows Wei-Chen's pain and vulnerability at the end of the narrative through the loaded image of the monkey which further complicates what we are to do with Jin Wang's equation with the Monkey King himself. Wei-Chen's presence at the end of the narrative is necessary for the reconciliation story and for Jin's self-acceptance, but Wei-Chen's "salvation" comes only when we and Jin, focalized through Jin Wang, see him as a vulnerable, pitiable, cute monkey. Are we to feel the pity that only one in a superior position can offer? Are we glad that the two little monkeys have found each other and are safely sharing tea in a culturally appropriate restaurant at story's end?

The use of the Monkey King's story of self-realization as a parallel narrative to Jin Wang's puts Gene Yang in a bind at the end of the novel. If we take the parallel to be absolute, Jin is to make his peace with the fact that he is a lesser human as the Monkey King is a lesser deity and that it begins and ends with race. The conclusion is that one is to be content as both separate and unequal and that this is a divine arrangement. Be yourself. Apparently, Jin can't be himself while dating Amelia, developing friendships with white kids, or playing on the school basketball team because, well, that's for white kids. A web board discussion devoted to *American Born Chinese*, which Yang cites in his Printz Award speech, included a person confessing, "I didn't want to be a person who had ADHD, I wanted to be normal and I kept trying to find a way to do it, I searched for a few years, but couldn't find a way to do it. Finally, I guess I just had to accept just who and what I was. Unfortunately, this urge still comes to me once in a great while." This person identifies the goal as "being normal." He or she also sets up a dichotomy between "people with

ADHD" and people who are "normal" as opposed to "everyone has a problem or condition that pushes us outside of normal." If there are ADHD kids in *American Born Chinese*, we don't see them. The kid with ADHD also fails to explain what the implications are for accepting himself as "abnormal."

To be fair to Yang, it *matters* that we consider Danny as figurative and Jin's self-delusion and that the Monkey King "awakens him" from a dream—a bad portal fantasy. Yang means for us to see the Monkey King as a sort of salvation: he returns Jin's soul to him. Yang's narrative is squarely focused more on cautioning the reader to be honest about who she is than on offering some sort of hope for transcendence or a way to be in the larger world, as these other critics have echoed. Writing about *American Born Chinese*, Jonathan Doughty says that the novel reminds us about a paradox: "Is identity one's possession or one's possessor? Or, rather: How do we possess our identities, and how do they possess us?" (60). Yang wants the reader to see Danny as a sort of demon possession. The ending has Jin in possession of himself. As a YA novel, a genre that tends to offer hopeful rather than happy endings, this book offers the reader a protagonist who is no longer what the narrative considers self-deluded and able to make choices from a position of honest self-perception. It feels hopeful. It isn't Yang who has created a peripheral existence for Jin Wang, after all, but the culture in which he is set by Yang's narrative. Clearly, Jin has a developed double consciousness—the ability to look at himself through the eyes of others—and can now decide what to do with that. Yang makes it clear, however, that adopting the viewpoint of others is not an acceptable option, and there is no real estate between selling out and bowing out. This is odd terrain for YA fiction, which tends to seek a way for the protagonist to be in the world. Robyn McCallum describes that adolescent tradition as one in which "central characters are represented as internally fragmented and/or solipsistic, and their stories articulate a quest for a sense of identity which is stable, coherent, unique and whole" (68). The form requires the assumption of a "singular and essential self [. . .] which underlies a person's own sense of, or more specifically desire for, a single and stable personal identity within, and relation to, the world and to others" (68). The relation to the world for Jin is, well, segregation. That Yang employs doubles—animal, mechanistic, racially other—may simply be his strategy of representing a developmental process (77). That development is seen at what can be argued to be the story's real ending: the almost postnarrative representation of a video still-shot in which Wei-Chen and Jin Wang are singing. This image is meant to call to mind a YouTube video by the "back dorm boys" who operate in spite of race without denying it. It is a form of appropriation that neither celebrates race nor makes it central. Race will always be with you, but there are ways to carve out a space. I can't show you the happy ending, Yang seems to say, but I can tell you that it isn't possible (whatever that ends up being) if you are in denial about yourself.

Yang's narrative can be acquitted of the accusations of complete hopelessness and second-class advocacy, but the endings of both the main narrative and the visual YouTube reference feel too ambiguous (and ephemeral) given the narrative weight and momentum of the twin narratives of Jin and the Monkey King that have accrued behind it. It remains ethically and narratologically ambiguous when clarity is essential for such a high-stakes novel of racial identity. As it is with books like *Harry Potter and the Sorcerer's Stone* or *Ella Enchanted*, Yang's book provides a vague sense of resolution for which the reader is simultaneously grateful and unsure about how it actually works as a resolution. It does not bear up under scrutiny. We are simply relieved that things work out in *some* way that sets things right. While the narrative implies that racial denial is simply unacceptable, and makes a case for moving forward, it doesn't show us what moving forward looks like, which strikes me as much more important in this novel than in novels generally. The Monkey King may offer Jin Wang acceptance of his racial identity, but Jin is left with really nothing but his racial identity. Is the choice of Danny as race erasure as laughable to the other students as Chin-key, the overethnicized option? Jin is the middle option between Danny and Chin-key, the realistic character in realism, but while the novel makes clear that neither race-erasing delusion nor laughable stereotype are acceptable options, we are still left with Jin Wang's question: "So what am I supposed to do now?"

The memory of a character's realness can only demean and make pathetic the character made increasingly more warped. It's a move that hasn't an upside, unlike the move from the real to the unreal. Such a transition, unlike the stable exaggerated character who is ridiculous from the start, suggests the likely presence of modes that we don't tend to want children to experience: irony and tragedy. The move toward the comically exaggerated, the pathetic, even the folkloric simplicity results in the feeling of loss in the reader. Junie B. Jones doesn't fill us with loss, but Jerry Renault does, and it has everything to do with the rhetorical move of modulation.

4

No Man's Land

Diagram 4

Between the Awesome and Absurd

This part of the character dial is where empathy goes to die in books, movies, and television shows for the young. Here we are not to seek ourselves in character, to see the real or sympathy-inducing other, or even to have that pity evoked for the pathetic. Between the larger than life and the smaller than life is not the life sized but the absence of anything lifelike. When the author dials or modulates the character from one extreme in this continuum toward the other, she is signaling to the reader that the combination of largeness and smallness will render in the balance not the life-sized character but an emotionless combination of absurdity and grandiosity.

It is an interesting rhetorical reality about character: there is a space between the larger-than-life and the smaller-than-life character that isn't life sized, that doesn't allow for the reader to see the character as worthy of sympathy much less offering identification by recognition. This is more of a no-man's-land caught the furthest distance away from sympathy, and therefore is ironically what many writers for children consider the safest place for a young reader to be. When an author wants to create a character that is entertaining without requiring of the reader an opportunity for sympathy—and hence engaging the vulnerable reader's emotions—this is the perfect modulation. We could call it the form of character modulation that is the concession to parental fear and authorial worries.

If we think about the particular children's medium of television and film cartoon, the propensity for this medium to give us combinations of silliness and awesomeness is noteworthy. I would argue that children's television cartoons are much more likely to provide the customer—the parent—a place to plunk the child down without worrying about any interruptions that might come from any ensuing emotional response from the child viewer, and the medium is also the perfect visual presentation of that combination. Dinner won't make itself, after all, and we need to have a video babysitter that will allow us a half hour to get the pot roast in the oven. If we consider such characters, whether "good" or "bad" (for it makes little difference), they provide the reader simultaneously low and high mimetic characters that inspire neither real fear nor admiration, although they certainly excite. Such television creations as the eponymous Fairly Odd Parents, *The Smurfs*' Gargamel, or *Phineas and Ferb*'s Dr. Doofenshmirtz offer us the titillation of the larger-than-life character (Fairies and evil scientists) but with an important neutralizer in the form of their absurdly comic representation. The funny mad scientist is the ultimate expression of this laughable grandeur. These characters can't become truly sympathetic without being dialed to one extreme of larger or smaller than life and then toward the life sized and real, and that's a great deal to ask of a reader. A character modulated between the larger and smaller than life presents us with false danger. When Gargamel or Wiley

E. Coyote (*super* genius) fail—and they most always do—and are subsequently sad, we laugh at them, which would be beastly behavior in any other context. This, it seems to me, is different than the laughter we aim at Junie B. Jones or Ramona the Pest, both of which are able to elicit real sympathy from us if not the extreme empathy of a life-sized, identifiable character. Junie B. and Ramona have a grain of humanity in them. We laugh at Ramona and, if we're from the south, express "bless her heart" as a follow up. This is different from the relieved and triumphant laughter at the failure of a funny baddie, little more than a video game villain. While pity is possible at the farthest reaches from the lifelike on either end of the scale of dimension, here on the opposite side of the dial from the lifelike the least sympathetically real and the most emotionally "safe" place for the child reader or viewer.

What do I mean by safe? It's the safety of distance created between reader and character, between the reader and sympathy. When Wile E. Coyote falls from a great height or is crushed by an anvil, we aren't fazed by the violence because there has been no room made for sympathy for these characters.[1] This is perhaps the most compelling defense for a certain sort of violence in children's media. When we see a character like Tom of *Tom and Jerry* get diced into pieces, it isn't happening to a character the author has given the reader the slightest sign that sympathy is owed. Absurd baddies like Disney's Gaston can fall from great heights and be forgotten the next second, whereas, ironically, when the Beast—who begins the story as a "bad guy"—is hurt, we feel sadness. The larger-than-life Beast has been made more real over the course of the narrative. We are moved from pity to sympathy. Gaston's death, in contrast, is the death of a character without the humanity that even the Beast has; it is the death of one for whom the author has denied us pity.[2] It is safe even to cheer his death, something we can only do when humanity has been denied.

The movement on this continuum between the larger and smaller than life is, unlike that found in chapters 2 and 3, a one-way modulation. An author can only modulate a character from the awesome to the laughable. This is the modulation made largely to defang the fearsome without asking for fellow feeling. While characters seem to be able to be made more sympathetic from the position of the absurd, they can't move immediately toward grandeur. It's a trick too hard to pull off. Moving a character decidedly absurd toward some sort of awesome status, I argue, is too much for an author to achieve.

Moving from Fearsome to Funny

One direction from the larger than life is toward the sympathetic and life sized, as discussed in chapter 2. Here instead I consider the implications for modulation from awesome to absurd. In this rhetorical context, the author has decided to reduce the character from grandeur but to make it absurd rather than sympathetic. As I discuss in chapter 2, the character Voldemort is modulated by Rowling through backstory to become more human for the reader in order to evoke some sympathy for him. At the very end of the series, however, she draws him back toward larger-than-life evil only to dial him further away from the life-sized and even fearsome evil to show him as a shriveled soul. When Harry is struck down by Voldemort and believes himself dead, he shows up in some version of King's Cross Station, neither clearly outside of his head nor an afterlife staging area. There he encounters what he does not know yet to be a fragment of Voldemort's soul that had been snuffed out by Voldemort himself: "It had the form of a small, naked child, curled on the ground, its skin raw and rough, flayed-looking, and it lay shuddering under a seat where it had been left, unwanted, stuffed out of sight, struggling for breath" (*Deathly Hallows* 706–07). Voldemort never recovers as a character from this image that Rowling creates in the mind of the reader, and the film depiction is especially devastating for any vision of Voldemort as larger than life without some tincture of pitiable contempt. He is shortly thereafter deprived of his penultimate sliver of soul when Neville Longbottom dispatches Nagini (733). Finally, he is seen desperately afraid and small, his hand "trembling on the Elder Wand" (742), and reduced to ridiculousness. After inviting us to sympathize with orphan Tom Riddle in order to awaken sympathy in the reader, Rowling pulls back and pivots/modulates toward the absurd. The gesture toward sympathy is short lived. Rowling reels him back toward larger-than-life evil again in order to redirect him along another line of modulation—one that denies sympathy.

In an earlier Rowling novel—*Harry Potter and the Prisoner of Azkaban*—we get a glimpse of how to make the fearsome into something funny. In chapter 7, the gang is introduced by Professor Lupin to a spell for defense against boggarts, creatures that assume the shape of your worst fear: "The charm that repels a boggart is simple, yet it requires force of mind. You see, the thing that really finishes a boggart is *laughter*. What you need to do is force it to assume a shape that you find amusing" (134). This sort of bending of a fearsome shape into something laughable is character modulation. The author announces with force of mind, "*Riddikulus!*" and the character that had been so fearsome is now deflated, and where before other characters had been cowed by it, they now crow over it. We see it in *The Lion, the Witch, and the Wardrobe* as a progression of scenes undercutting the character of the White Witch, previously so very fearsome to Edmund and others. When the White Witch has Edmund in tow as she searches for his siblings, she encounters a party of animals. When they claim to have been given their provisions by Father Christmas, the witch does not embrace the challenge of invasion but is shown to be weak by denying it: "He has not been here! He cannot have been here! How dare you—but no. Say you have been lying and you shall even now be forgiven" (127). She is then made to suffer the indignity of having to abandon her sleigh and trudge through the mud, as Aslan's influence has been thawing out Narnia, until now under the witch's thrall. When presented with this theory that Aslan is the cause of this thaw, she threatens to kill the next person to mention "that name" (133), showing her to be shaken by his very invocation. Her threats come from weakness, smallness, ridiculousness, and the ignorant denial of lion-made climate change. When the witch secures the promise from Aslan that he will sacrifice himself for Edmund, she asks him, "But how do I know this promise will be kept?" and is met with a roar from

Aslan. This leaves the witch "staring for a moment with her lips wide apart," and she "picked up her skirts and fairly ran for her life" (158). The image, and now this witch, is broadly comic. Earlier in the story, the witch and Aslan are perched at what seems to be the extreme of larger than life, but before he is dialed toward sympathy through his willingness to be sacrificed—the god made man—she is shown to be someone who can be frightened by Aslan, and she is the god made small without the benefit of sympathy. It is as if Aslan—and by extension Lewis—yells "*Riddikulus!*" at the White Witch, and she turns into a scornful little girl long enough for us to wonder why we fear her, and she never recovers.

The key to this modulation, however, is that the character begins by being actually fearsome—truly larger than life. When a character is made to sit at the extreme position of larger than life, it is for the moment full of the potential for modulation: it has potential to remain fearsome and distant, to be modulated toward sympathy and life-sized humanity, or to be made ridiculous by degrees or all at once. For there to be movement and not stasis of character, the author has to modulate in one of two directions: pathos or bathos. The modulation of the witch toward smallness is often accomplished by having someone presumptuous and *small* challenge her, which further compounds the effect of making the witch ridiculous rather than fearsome—something that the small can actually defeat, and sometimes without a great deal of effort. This for obvious reasons happens in children's literature quite a lot. Unlike with the modulation toward sympathy from either the larger than life or smaller than life, the move from the awesome to the ridiculous can happen quite suddenly. The Wicked Witch of the West needs only a short bath, delivered by a little girl, to reduce her to a pile of clothes. In one moment, she is ready to destroy Dorothy and her friends, and the next, she is reduced to laundry. It's one of the stranger plot moves in classic children's literature, granted, but we accept it because we're desperate for Dorothy. Contrived? Yes. It's ridiculous, unearned, and unexplained, but the ridiculousness of the action and the effect is enormously bathetic. This is not an ending that results from a great battle against a great warrior, as Maleficent's death is, although even she is defeated by a smaller, weaker foe—it's a dousing with a bucket of water by a young girl who is already the witch's prisoner.

Early in chapter 12, after the Scarecrow tells the Guardian of the Gates of Oz that his group plans on destroying the Wicked Witch of the West, the Guardian observes, "No one has ever destroyed her before, so I naturally thought she would make slaves of you, as she has of all the rest. But take care; for she is wicked and fierce" (140). The witch is clearly afraid of Dorothy when she is brought by the flying monkeys. She has the mark of Glinda and the Silver Shoes, so the witch "began to tremble with fear" (150). She is made ridiculous before the girl who shows little ability to defeat her. Despite this, Dorothy is made a slave. When one day Dorothy is made angry by the witch, the girl "picked up the bucket of water that stood near and dashed it over the Witch, wetting her from head to foot" (154). Crying out in fear, the witch confesses that "in a minute I shall melt away" (154). As strange and as random as this is, the witch is made even more ridiculous by asking the question, "Didn't you know water would be the end of me?" in a "wailing, despairing voice" (154). As if to echo the reader's thoughts, Dorothy says, "Of course not. How should I?" That such a figure would ask such a question in a castle that has buckets of water for easy use is the height of stupid, and she melts with this thought in our minds.

In the recent Newbery novel, *The Girl Who Drank the Moon*, we see another deflation of the larger than life to the absurd. It is the story of the Sorrow Eater who has assumed the name Sister Ignatia and who has fed off of the carefully designed misery of a community for five hundred years. She is built up to be an extraordinary power and foe. In the end, she is knocked off her perch by being reduced to a sad girl by a little girl. Just as this Sorrow Eater is prepared to destroy Luna, Xan, the madwoman, and Antain at story's end, Luna uses her magic to look deep "in the space where the Sorrow Eater's heart should have been" and finds "a tiny sphere—hard, shiny, and cold. A pearl" (362). It is her reduced heart that has sealed off all of her memory at losing her own family when she was a child. She had become a monstrous sorrow eater to fill the void in herself, so she created sorrow to feed on. In an instant, Luna opens the pearl of her heart, the woman is drained of life, spilling sorrow all around, ages her full five hundred years, and dies. The Sorrow Eater is larger-than-life powerful and immortal one moment and then revealed to be a little girl who is too weak to choose love over power, as Xan puts it (364). She dies a dried husk all in a few moments. Like the Witch of the West, she is deflated, dissolved.

In Nnedi Okarafor's *Akata Witch*, the ensemble protagonists Sunny, Orlu, Sasha, and Chici—teenagers not older than fifteen—are chosen to by their own Leopard People, magical people on Earth, to defeat the Black Hat, an agent of a great evil power, a fourth-level wielder of magic. An expert, the elder Abok, tells the children: "He is master; he is powerful. But something went wrong, and now he is corrupt, too" (308). He is a killer who plans on slaughtering two toddlers to create the magic necessary to bring his master, Ekwensu, into the world. The children are told it is they who must stop him. They fail to stop the Black Hat, and Ekwensu—whom Chici describes as "what Satan is to the Christians. [. . .] But more real, more tangible. She's not a metaphor or a symbol" (312)—enters the world. As the larger-than-life Ekwensu take physical shape in the world, dancing and enjoying the sensation of corporeality, the girl Sunny approaches her. It all happens fast, and strikes us as well as Ekwensu as absurdly anticlimactic. Sunny makes some gestures with her magical juju knife and simply says the word "Return," and Ekwensu starts to spin, diminish, and sink. In a telling description, the narrator tells us that as Sunny "watched Ekwensu sink, she was reminded of the Wicked Witch of the West's death in The Wizard of Oz. Ekwensu wasn't melting, but she looked like she was, as she sank into the wet, red mud. Gone" (327). The powerful spirit is smacked down by a child, and the suddenness and absurdity of it is striking. Okorafor invokes the death of the Witch of the West directly to reinforce the modulation of character. A being feared throughout the book is taken out by a child with a simple gesture. The ease of its defeat makes Ekwensu absurd, and even in the second novel, *Akata Warrior*, when it returns to battle Sunny, it can never be as large as it was before its initial defeat.

The Grand High Witch in Roald Dahl's popular book *The Witches* has her own absurd comeuppance. Dahl devotes almost a third of his novel to a meeting of witches held in the Hotel Magnificent in Bournemouth where our protagonist and his grandmother are having holiday.[3] For sixty pages, the Grand High Witch holds court over all the witches in England, and it is clear that she is not only to be feared by humanity, but all of the witches themselves live in fear of her temper. One witch is "frizzled like a fritter" for speaking out of turn. After being turned into a mouse after being given a dose of "Formula 86," a "delayed action mouse-maker," our young hero escapes the ballroom full of witches, steals a whole vial of Formula 86 from the Grand High Witch's room, and manages to pour the contents into the soup tureen from which all of the witches will sup that evening. The Grand High Witch isn't even singled out but is part of the general absurdity of witches turning into mice: "In another few seconds, all the witches had completely disappeared and the tops of the two long tables were swarming with small brown mice" (186). The Grand High Witch is not only made absurd but is made absurd by a boy, and a boy who has himself been turned into a mouse.

Of course, the world of children's stories is populated by many bullies, and the bully—a larger-than-life figure among children—can experience the three modulations that any larger-than-life character can experience: a turn toward sympathy, stasis as larger-than-life, or a turn toward the absurd. Bullies can be adults or children. Some of Roald Dahl's other books feature such bullies. We see the objectionable aunts (Spiker and Sponge) quashed by an enormous peach in *James and the Giant Peach*, reduced to an absurd smear by a large fruit when moments before they were larger-than-life monsters in James's life. The infamous Miss Trunchbull, headmistress of Crunchem Hall Primary School, is shown to be a frightened and pathetic adult when the eponymous Matilda uses her telekinetic powers to convince Trunchbull that the ghost of her uncle is out to get her. Roald Dahl always opts for this third option with larger-than-life villains; he isn't interested in giving children reformed or undefeatable villains.[4] He wants baddies purely unsympathetic and made foolish by the end.

A famous bully, and deadly one at that, defeated in comic and absurd fashion—and by the ultimate forever child—is Captain James Hook. Near the end of Hook's time in the story, the narrator notes of him that "misguided man though he was, we may be glad, without sympathizing with him, that in the end he was true to the traditions of his race" (208). He is described as striking at the boys "impotently" and hoping to catch Peter in bad form at the last. Before jumping from the ship, absurdly into the waiting jaws of the crocodile that continuously, ridiculously stalks him, he is glad to catch Peter kicking at him rather than using his blade and jumps content, yelling "Bad form" (209). It is an absurd image and end to the larger-than-life villain of *Peter Pan*. The narrator has even been careful to remind us not to feel sympathy, which is unnecessary. We don't. We shake our heads in disgust. Why were we ever afraid of Captain Hook?

One implication of keeping whole categories of character larger than life in a static condition is that their failure to evoke either sympathy through being made lifelike or even pity through becoming absurd is that they are no more than cannon fodder. We see an extreme example of this in the Lord of the Rings movies, in which Legolas and Gimli compete for killing the most orcs, rattling off their kill count as they dispatch nameless orcs one after another. Fantasy is especially rife with this larger-than-life horde of evil that can be eliminated without a single ethical qualm. Zombies are an especially popular form of this in today's films and television shows, but we have Star Wars storm troopers and the cauldron born in Lloyd Alexander's Prydain books to add to this list. It carries over to realism and propaganda pretty readily in movies and books for children over the years, including any foes of the British Isles, Nazis, Native Americans, and more. The static, larger-than-life foe can be singular like the Grand High Witch or Sauron, or that figure can simply be a placeholder for the bad guy, and the failure of the author to turn the dial, to mediate toward sympathy or pity, means that they are disposable. They provide the author figures who can't hold any emotional charge for the reader and are useful for certain purposes, all of which should give us pause.

Moving toward the Grandiose?

This direction, of all six outlined, is the one least possible. In fact, I can't come up with examples of a character being modulated from the smaller than life to the larger than life without moving through the life sized or sympathetic. Even little mice like Despereaux and Stuart Little—small and unremarkable in the beginning and heroic by the end—are objects of sympathy over the course of their stories. The smaller than life turned hero takes the long way around the dial, having to be made sympathetic and loved on the way toward big things. The idea of modulating absurd, comic characters toward larger-than-life grandeur is where the issue of plausibility is strained the most, and someone like Lloyd Alexander will have to take a Gurgi the long way around. There is simply no shortcut from the absurd to the awe-inspiring, unlike what we've seen above regarding making the awesome absurd. That drop off is possible; the climb is too much. A character like Voldemort who can be made more sympathetic through back story can be dialed back toward larger than life and even then toward the absurd at the end; a character larger than life made absurd can't be made awesome again. We won't have it. Once dialed to the absurd from the awesome, the plunging door latch won't let the author dial back the other way. There would be no way back but onward toward the sympathetic portrayal of the lifelike.

What does it mean that there is a modulation that is emotionally unattainable? I have shown how the creators of many different texts for young readers modulate character toward and away from sympathy and different forms of "realness." It seems that there are many different tools for and examples of oscillations from the awesome to the sympathetic to the absurd and back again. The movement from the awesome directly to the absurd is often achieved as a precipitous drop as though a once-and-for-all concession of status. The reverse direction is forsaken. A character in that space between the awesome and absurd can only slide, lose ground. Once at the bottom, it can be modulated back around toward sympathy, because while it seems that loss of status can be attained without pity, gaining it can't be. There is no way from the absurd to the awesome except through sympathy. C. S. Lewis shows us the folly of this attempt by a character trying to modulate another character. When the ape Shift tries to gain control over Narnia, he believes his best bet is to offer up a false Aslan as an alternative to Aslan himself. He manages to convince Puzzle, a donkey, to put on the skin of a Lion and pretend to be the great lion. Puzzle comes to his senses and joins up with Jill and Eustace in their efforts to right things in the kingdom. Puzzle returns to a position he never really left. Lewis doesn't actually modulate Puzzle; Shift is shown to pretend to. Whether this is some sort of emotional message authors universally demand for children's characters or some sort of rule of literary physics, I can't say. It is reassuring that the absurd, if it ascends to some sort of power through hook or crook and not through an appeal to a shared, sympathetic humanity remains an emperor without clothes, a false king, a propped-up puppet, a charlatan. It's reassuring that authors for children reassert that truth to their readers.

Conclusion

The rhetorical modulation of character in literature for the young as I have envisioned it has five viable directions, and in each of those modulations a decision is made by an author to invite, foster, and often change an emotional relationship between character and reader as it regards sympathy. Characters can be made larger than life, smaller than life, or sympathetic (life sized). Sympathetic characters can be dialed toward the awesome or the absurd; larger-than-life characters can be made more sympathetic or absurd; the smaller-than-life character can be made more sympathetic. Examining how and why authors make such modulations offers one way to understand the emotional manipulation of young readers through story. For this reason, such a study is of value to those studying the ethics of children's literature. Can writers for the young eschew authority and responsibility for the ways that they modulate character? What are the ethical implications for modulation of characters that depict people of color, the differently abled, or people of various religious traditions in the direction of the smaller or larger than life or away from or toward sympathy from either of these positions? While I address issues of race and diversity, there is easily a book-length project applying this idea of rhetorical modulation of character to the representation of race and culture in very specific instances. Does this rhetorical model hold any value for those studying Greek children's books or books that represent Korean children in Anglophone literature for children? I don't know, but I hope and expect so. It may be that such applications point out implications for this sort of rhetorical approach that I haven't anticipated.

Rhetorical modulation can be considered for the purpose of speculating on the ultimate destination of character in a narrative. Will this story adhere to modal expectations and keep character from modulating at all? Will character shift toward grandeur, and how far, and after having established what sorts of sympathies if any? Can we read with critical suspicion the character who has shown tendencies toward the absurd while still larger than life, and what might provoke a descent into the absurd? Reading with an eye toward modulation away from or toward reader sympathy gives us a tool for predicting character change based on what an author has already established regarding our distance from that character. Is the author pulling us closer to character, establishing protective distance, or balancing the acts of keeping us in reach yet holding us at arm's length? The anthropomorphic character is the epitome of that tension, and I have discussed its ambiguous and debated function as a tool for immersion and protection simultaneously. As the anthropomorphic character serves as a metaphor for that tension, the dial of modulation provides a metaphor for the movement of such characters through stories that we give the young.

I examine the role of media in this rhetorical model, but it isn't a primary focus. What are the implications for character modulations specifically in forms like the graphic novel, picture book, prose novel, verse novel, television program, film, and more? Do modulations happen differently, with more or less regularity, with greater or lesser impact on the emotional response of the reader in different media? A focused study on medium would likely point to the special techniques used to establish sympathy.

A rhetorical consideration of character might be extended with more affective critical tools. Can studies in reader response or cognitive narratology offer up a new insight by considering the reader's end of the rhetorical exchange of character modulation?

Does character modulation happen with a different purpose or with different techniques in earlier literatures for children? I mention in chapter 3 the function of character modulation in cautionary young adult (YA) literature; is the tradition of the cautionary tale—the nineteenth-century Sunday school story, for instance—a fruitful place to study such modulations in more depth? Do authors offer character modulation between larger- and smaller-than-life characters in early twentieth-century France? I expect that while such studies will show the limitations of this rhetorical approach, we may be surprised to find that it reveals something about authorial manipulation instead. I hope so.

It's possible that you've disagreed with a reading of a modulation somewhere in this volume. That's inevitable. It's my hope that while you might object to a claim I make about the direction a character is modulated that you find the framework, the idea of the rhetorical modulation, useful. We can disagree about the direction a character is modulated while agreeing that the idea itself is useful and interesting.

I began this discussion by pointing to Doctor Dolittle's friend the pushmi-pullyu, a creature living under the necessary tension between coming and going. I want to end with invoking that image again. A consideration of the rhetorical modulation of character in literature for the young points out the necessary, natural tensions present in the stories adults tell for children. We simultaneously want the child reader to become immersed and to be protected, to be engaged and to be safe. Since the degree to which characters are sympathetic is key to our emotional response to them, authors will modulate that sympathy in character construction over the course of a story or series of stories.

Notes

Introduction

1. See Andrea Schwenke Wyile's article "Expanding the View of First-Person Narration" for a discussion of how picture books engage and distance. In that article she claims that most children's narration is engaging rather than distancing.

2. Aidan Chambers warns us to "be wary of using as evidence in criticism what an author says about himself, publicly or privately: a caution we have not sufficiently taken to heart in talking about children's books" (98). For my purposes, authorial commentary serves as a way to illustrate the different ways authors think about their relationship to their texts, audiences, and genre rather than using authorial commentary as a way to validate a particular view or reading.

3. While Walsh echoes Wimsatt and Beardsley's concern over a reaction to "using the text to comment on the author," she, as author, feels the authority to comment on her own text. The other children's authors also comment on the text but in terms of the text's role in communicating to an audience rather than as a measure of a text's independent meaning.

4. Wayne Booth points out, quite rightly, that "we can no longer pretend that ethical criticism is passé. It is practically everywhere, often surreptitiously, often guiltily, and often badly" (*The Company We Keep* 19).

5. Though my focus is on a rhetorical conception of child readers held by children's writers, critics in children's literature and childhood studies have weighed in on the theoretical concept as well as real reader—often in the service of trying to determine whether a book is for children or not. While this is fascinating, and a tempting route to follow, it is an endless and for me here derivative path, however worthwhile. Jacqueline Rose's 1984 *The Case of Peter Pan: The Impossibility of Children's Literature*, and Aidan Chambers's 1985 *Book Talk: Occasional Writing on Literature for Children* (especially the chapter "The Reader in the Book") are two early and provocative discussions on the relative usefulness, possibility, and categorical nature of children's audience. Perry Nodelman's 2008 *The Hidden Adult*

and Marah Gubar's 2011 *PMLA* article "On Not Defining Children's Literature" are two more recent forays into this question of taxonomy. Scholars Karen Coats, Richard Flynn, and Mary Galbraith come at the issue from a childhood studies point of view. In his piece, Flynn decries the simple binaries of adult/child distinctions and calls for a critical investigation into childhood "often experienced more in memory than in actuality" (143); Coats warns against generalizing about "the child" in ways that cause us to "set aside specific cultural, ethnic, embodied conditions that have real effects on the ways that children perceive and interact with their worlds" (140); Galbraith lauds postmodern critiques of childhood for "promoting methodological skepticism about 'the real child'" (199).

6. There is mutuality in this rhetorical situation. Ethicist and children's author/scholar Claudia Mills agrees with James Phelan about the need for rhetorical responsibility by both author and reader. Because the author has decided to guide the reader in a particular way, it is the reader's responsibility to consider that choice (*Experiencing Fiction* ix). Mills argues that "just as writers must exercise ethical responsibility in how they write, readers must exercise ethical responsibility in how they read" (10).

Chapter 1

1. Elizabeth Segel decries genre's equation with mimesis. She points out that "one is first struck by the absolute incompatibility between the aims of most writers for children and the aims of the realistic school" (417) and goes on to say that "the dismissal of fantasy as frivolous and immoral by educators of all persuasions prior to the mid-nineteenth century meant that in those years most books written specifically for children took as their subject every day events in contemporary settings. Yet they are certainly not examples of realism" (418). In fact, Maria Nikolajeva notes that "children's literature is historically a recent form of fiction. It's emergence in the eighteenth to nineteenth centuries coincides with the establishment of realism (mimetic modes) in the mainstream)" (*Rhetoric* 27). Ursula K. Le Guin points to "fake realism" ("Why Are Americans Afraid of Dragons?") and C. S. Lewis to "superficial realism" ("On Three Ways"), which are both ultimately forms of wish fulfillment in a realistic setting.

2. Maria Nikolajeva posits that "as mediators of literature we want children to be able to place themselves in other people's life situations" rather than simply see their own (in Cadden, *Telling Children's Stories* 205). She adds that "the conviction that young readers must adopt the subject position of a literary character is [. . .] totally ungrounded and in fact prevents the development of mature reading" (188). Barker observes that "most early children's books present characters as models for the reading child rather than as subjects of identification" (102)—they were to learn from characters' behaviors only. Character became for all ages of readers much more

psychologically rich and round through the nineteenth century. The twentieth century introduced the movement from didactic modeling to identification, though.

3. Moira Hinderer claims regarding the development of the Black character in twentieth-century American children's books that "authors, teachers, and librarians argued that adults had an ethical obligation to provide Black children with more realistic descriptions of children like themselves" (52).

4. Character dimension is "any attribute a character may be said to possess when that character is considered in isolation from the work in which he or she appears," whereas character function "is a particular application of that attribute made by the text through its developing structure" (Phelan, *Reading People, Reading Plots* 9). "Dimensions are converted to functions by the *progression* of the work" (Phelan, *Reading People, Reading Plots* 9). I am interested in function rather than in dimension (what the character does rather than details that enrich them).

5. The anthropomorphic character is almost equally important, and the anthropomorphic character might be a child as well.

Chapter 2

1. When Harry and Dumbledore use the Pensieve to watch Dumbledore's first meeting with eleven-year-old Tom Riddle, Harry is struck with how quickly Tom accepts the news that he's a wizard. "He believed it much quicker than I did" (276). Dumbledore remarks that "Riddle was perfectly ready to believe that he was—to use his word—'special'" (276). This, both Dumbledore and we know, is not the mark of the sympathetic character.

2. Glenna Sloan's *The Child as Critic* is the most thorough application of Frye's work in the context of children's literature.

3. Moira Hinderer verifies that most "early children's books present characters as models for the reading child rather than as subjects of identification" (Hinderer 102). We were meant to learn from them rather than emotionally engage. Michael Levy and Farah Mendlesohn point out that the "children of fantasy prior to 1950 *were children*. Those afterwards were, as Susan Cooper named Will Stanton, *Old Ones*, simultaneously children and carriers of adult responsibilities who looked beyond themselves; and this has continued to the present day" (108).

4. Nikolajeva rightly points out that Frye's ironic character includes in Frye's own list of inferior characters the disabled, animals, and children (*Rhetoric* 26), so it would seem that his list isn't applicable to the study of children's literature. If we simply acknowledge that Frye's imagination, though educated, is limited in terms of how children can be depicted in children's books, we can expand the roles children play in their own literature.

5. Martha Hixon describes character as "descriptive phrases, bits of dialogue, moments of action that forward the plot" (256). Karen Coats argues that "literary

characters are made of ink and ideas, after all, but we do treat them as though there were real . . ." (Bloomsbury 194). Maria Nikolajeva shares that she finds "it of overall importance to remind ourselves and our students that literary characters are indeed constructions, fictitious figures and not actual human beings" (Rhetoric 19).

6. See my "The Irony of Narration in the Young Adult Novel."

7. In fact, Le Guin modulates in the original Earthsea trilogy. Ged begins somewhat unreal and unsympathetic—a child prodigy with little empathy for others himself. That continues until he looses the Shadow upon the world, which both injures and humbles him, drawing him toward the real as a figure of sympathy (if not merely pity). His subsequent triumph returns him to the unreal but dragging the sympathy which he's earned, the ultimate prize of character modulation. He then experiences a second humbling when his powers are lost in his defeat of Cobb. *Tehanu* begins in the reverse form of the original trilogy with Ged as humble and real, but he drags his glory with him from the first trilogy. Le Guin has modulated Ged several times to manipulate our emotional attachment to him. It's not about his growth but about his rhetorical use in the narrative.

8. It's interesting to wonder to what extent autobiographies by authors serve as a form of backstory. These provide for the reader familiar with a "character" like Gary Paulsen or Jacqueline Woodson a background to their ultimate success. Paulsen's *Woodsong* validates the legitimacy of the author's fiction, and Woodson's *Brown Girl Dreaming* provides explanation for her interest in story and poetry.

9. Ponyboy is typical of another character move that has modulation implications. Like Wilbur from *Charlotte's Web* and Jesse Aarons in *Bridge to Terabithia*, Ponyboy is the character who survives and benefits, while the "twin" character dies. This modulates the character in two ways: it creates sympathy for their loss while it keeps them as beneficiary of that loss, a somewhat exalted status. See my "Simultaneous Emotions: Entwining Modes in Children's Books."

10. Home-away-home as a defining feature of children's books is discussed in such works as Clausen, Stott, Stott and Francis, Cadden ("Purposeful Movement," "Home Is a Matter of Blood"), Nodelman, and Reimer. Maria Nikolajeva discusses the importance of the chronotope in children's literature, especially as a trans-genre phenomenon equally at home in realism as fantasy. The secondary chronotope—the portal world—in realism is more pronounced in space than time, she says, and is a tool for distinguishing "between sacred and profane space" (*Comes of Age* 130).

11. Along with those mentioned above, Bilbo Baggins, Lyra Belacqua, Sunny Nwazue, and Jerusha Abbott are characters who move into another world to be modulated. The modulation often happens with the assistance of helpers whose character function is largely to help the modulating protagonist (and us) navigate this world newly sprung upon them (and us).

12. Epilogues often work in this contrasting way, as either summative or scenic. For examples and a discussion of this, see my "All Is Well: The Epilogue in Children's Fantasy Fiction."

13. Maria Nikolajeva observes that "there seems to be a difference between genres in providing characters' background. In adventure stories, the background is often of no importance" (*Rhetoric* 22). While genre may account for part of it, she notes that it may have more to do with character-driven as opposed to plot-driven narrative, which can be a matter of genre (mystery as usually plot drive, for instance). I think it's less sure to point to those matters, though they are often good measures, than to observe when it's in the author's interest to manipulate character through the revelation of background.

14. J. K. Rowling is famous for adding backstory through the epitext of public commentary. Apart from the moves to identify Dumbledore as gay, for instance, she has added the "fact" that "Vernon's dislike for Harry 'stems in part, like Severus Snape's, from Harry's close resemblance to the father they both so disliked'" (Ross). It raises the question of whether backstory is "legitimate" coming from the author in epitextual ways in contrast to narrators informing readers from within the text. Arguably, Rowling is no more empowered to add to or change the narrative from the outside than we are. Marius Hentea points out that "because it can never be complete, there is a risk that back story can overwhelm the narrative, thus leading to calls for 'artistic economy'" (349). Because characters aren't people and have no life outside the text, providing them backstory in a context that is removed from the narrative isn't only irrelevant, it's sort of comic. Readers of the Harry Potter books don't necessarily have access to Rowling's comments about characters, so it has no impact on the narrative and the character's function in the narrative, which is the only real use of backstory. Critical speculation about character is derived from the text and the information an author provides; not only is authorial pronouncement of character "facts" after the story is over self-indulgent, but it's of no use.

15. Foreshadowing may be one of the most obvious and powerful of rhetorical moves in narrative. Foreshadowing offers the reader a clue to future information, and it implies of the reader an ability to recognize the rhetorical elbow to the ribs.

16. The boy and the grandmother are never named in the narrative.

17. The creation of a magical context for conflict or difference can serve to mask an otherwise mundane—though no less sympathetic—story. One of my favorite examples of this is the basis of the novel *Twilight*. The story of Edward and Bella can be told without the use of vampirism. Edward is someone worried that his lover might catch his condition, which causes him to have to abstain from contact with her, though he desperately wants that contact. She assures him that she doesn't want protection and, in fact, wants to prove her love for him by exposing herself to it. He can't bear the idea that she will be hurt by him, and she is hurt that he won't let her make her own choices. This could easily be the story of a couple wrestling with the problem of sexually transmitted disease, like herpes. Ironically, though this is a real and emotionally touching story acted out by thousands of teen couples in the world, my class routinely decides that this, not the story of vampirism, is ridiculous. Vampirism becomes a "romantic"

metaphor for something we don't want decoded. Instead of real characters with a real problem, the characters are made unreal (and undead) which somehow ennobles their problems.

18. See Kertzer. In the section "What Is Traumatic Memory? The Debates Outside Our Field," she draws on Richard J. McNally's critique of naive assumptions regarding flashbacks. McNally is a Harvard-based clinical psychologist who has written many books on traumatic memory.

19. Of course, this is tricky. Few readers involved in McKinley's novel won't know the story of Beauty already, so there is that epitextual presence. This is even truer now than it was in 1978 before the Disney movie. So, the question is whether the novel works on its own, or must, or whether it's naïve to expect that readers will not know what is coming. It is interesting to note that the Disney version provides the viewer the information about the prince in a prologue, in contrast to Beaumont's and McKinley's respective tales. The Disney audience, then, is assumed to not know the story and are implied to be people who would be horrified at Belle's falling in love with a big German shepherd, which is understandable. Disney, like McKinley, requires love, so the story would be unsettling if we didn't know the Beast was really a man. We are not to question why Belle, who doesn't know, is okay with it.

20. A recent remake of Cinderella makes a similar use of backstory. In her 2012 debut novel *Cinder*, Marissa Meyer has our heroine sympathetic as a cyborg in a world that doesn't grant cyborgs the status of full humanity. Our sympathy in full force following her terrible treatment by her stepmother and her courage to try to protect the prince from harm, we and she discover that she is actually the rightful queen of the moon. Instant Unreal status grounded in the affection of sympathy.

21. Some narratives for children are founded on the idea that growing up makes one unreal or not sympathetic to the child reader. To catch the contagion of aging, to be thought to be transitioning to adulthood, is often a deal breaker. Susan Pevensie, Wendy, Caddie Woodlawn—all of these young girls lose their stories—or their children's stories come to an end—when they become women. With the loss of childhood comes a loss of interest, concern, reality to the young reader, or so the author argues to the reader.

22. The television series *Once* is almost a comic series of recast characters achieved through endless and interconnected backstories.

23. My students are often split on the question of whether this provides adequate information to forgive Cecile. Those who are of the opinion that a mother doesn't leave her children under any circumstances aren't going to have their minds changed.

24. In the popular television show *The Big Bang Theory*, Sheldon Cooper is modulated from the beginning of the series onward from being wooden and without empathy to being, as his roommate Leonard has said, "a real live boy." The Pinocchio reference is telling. Science fiction is rife with examples of the

android seeking humanity, or the acceptance by humanity as real, including Isaac Asimov's *I, Robot*, Stanley Kubrick's *A. I. Artificial Intelligence*, and Philip K. Dick's *Do Androids Dream of Electric Sheep?*.

25. As Pinocchio is made human, the bad boys with whom he cavorts are turned into donkeys. They are bad, and they do not deserve our pity. They are pushed away from human society.

26. Ursula K. Le Guin's YA protagonists are all over the map of movement between the real and unreal. As Ged moves from unreal to real, enacting our sympathy, Tenar and Orrec are protagonists of different novels in which they go from ordinary children to feared adolescents only to regain their ordinariness at the end, and Ged moves in the opposite direction in his transition from *The Farthest Shore* to *Tehanu*—from Archmage to common man bereft of magic.

Chapter 3

1. One is reminded of Jessica Rabbit's lament: "I'm not bad. I'm just drawn that way." How one is drawn is an act of rhetoric that means to communicate something to the viewer/reader about that character.

2. Exaggeration is created by the author in order to disturb or amuse the reader in much the same way that visual artists create surreal or cartoon images for the same effects, respectively, on the viewer; and, just as some images can create a confused response in a viewer ("I can't tell whether it's funny in a disturbing way or disturbing in a funny way!"), the author of character can modulate character so the reader has an equally confused response. The author may want us to be disturbed or amused by a character but simultaneously sympathetic to keep us thinking about them, to challenge perceptions. This is especially true of YA literature. It's a risky move because it may lose for the reader any empathy capital built up with that character. I think there's more tension in the space between the real and the exaggerated than between real an unreal—there's more at risk, more potential confusion. The character who at times seems larger than life and at other times normal and sympathetic is less confusing than one with whom we don't know whether to laugh or cry. In other words, getting size right or consistent may be less difficult than getting the warp right.

3. Perry Nodelman's *Words about Pictures*, published in 1988, is the seminal text dealing with the ironic relationship between words and pictures in children's picture books. Painter and colleagues offer us in *Reading Visual Narratives* a social semiotic rather than art or literary theory approach, which is useful in a rhetorical approach.

4. Of course, artistic style can fluctuate even in the same text as it relates to character depiction—even the same character at different moments in the

narrative can be modulated to move from real to exaggerated to achieve the changed emotional effect on the reader sought by the author/illustrator. If we think only of illustrations rather than prose construction of character, there are countless examples of characters depicted realistically, though perhaps not as often as in other schools of art. Some illustrators specialize in realism, such as Beatrix Potter and Jerry Pinkney, but that obviously doesn't limit them to realism as a literary genre. Both Potter and Pinkney have written and illustrated a great deal of animal fantasy. In picture book texts, the written part of the narrative is necessarily brief, so it is the case that the illustrations carry most if not the entirety of the weight of the rhetoric of character.

5. Waber is the author/illustrator of the Lyle the Crocodile books as well, so his cartoon style still communicates the same exaggerated quality to character, but we are in animal fantasy in those books. Eve Bunting also writes about social justice using folk art, as in *Smoky Night*, a depiction of the Los Angeles riots following the Rodney King trial verdict and illustrated by David Diaz. This has a distancing effect from the violence for the reader. While Waber offers the same rhetorical relationship to readers regarding character through illustration, he does it across genre; Bunting can focus on the same genre but vary the distance between character and reader through shifting artistic style.

6. Painter, Martin, and Unsworth in a recent semiotic study of images in picture books point to the specific relationship between character and reader: "In a narrative text, the roles, relationships and affects realized through the interpersonal metafunction are not just those set up between reader and writer/image-maker on the one hand and those between the characters themselves on the other but also (crucially) involve those in play between the reader and the narrative characters" (15). They focus on the use of focalization, ambience, and the detailed semiotic relationships of what they call "unmediated," "mediated," "direct," "invited," and more (29). They place importance "on the basis of the degree of detail and realism of the drawing," as I do (31). Important to this study, they point to three broad character illustrated types: minimalist, generic, and naturalistic that offer degrees of empathetic response. I recommend their discussion of the pathos affect in illustration.

7. There are changes from the original novel to the film that have their own effects on character, of course. It's interesting to note that the Russell graphic novel offers through the depiction of the respective dialogue and narration boxes a verbatim account of the Gaiman novel, so the most profitable comparison might be between McKean's and Russell's respective versions.

8. Another example of the social modulation of character is in *Caddie Woodlawn*. Caddie is seen to become more real and life sized—ready to grow up. When she is told that her days as a tomboy are over and that she is to behave like a young lady, she is modulated from absurd "girl-boy" into a credible person.

9. Although different from folktale characters, the miniature character almost always has to move from a reduced state—literally—in the eyes of the child

protagonist toward a revised status of equal. By beginning the narrative with the child encountering a miniature character, the author establishes what seems an obvious hierarchy in sympathy for the reader and the child progatonist. Mary Norton's *The Borrowers* features Arietty Clock and her small family, who must convince the boy in the story that she is a person like him. Lynne Reid Banks' *The Indian in the Cupboard* depicts the movement of Little Bear from play thing to equal to adult superior to the boy Omri who calls Little Bear forth from a small cupboard. In the cases of *The Indian in the Cupboard* by Lynne Reid Banks and Mary Norton's *The Borrowers*, the miniature figures initially encountered by the children in the novel are seen as either toys or as a sort of vermin. After the initial shock of the encounter, the children in the respective novels, who are meant as highly sympathetic avatars for the child reader, learn to pity then sympathize, and even empathize with the small people. They are also shamed into it by the homunculi. The novels end with the small humans leaving the houses of the children—Little Bear and Boone back to their real places in history, and Arrietty and the Clock family into the world. By the end of each narrative, the small characters have been made real, sympathetic, no longer side-show freaks and objects but subjects worthy of consideration. Metaphorically, they are examples of how the child must see the others not as objects or things but as people, as subjects. Maria Nikolajeva argues that "animals, toys, baby witches, and animated objects are always disguises for a child" (*Rhetoric* 125). In the cases where modulation occurs, the disguise of their unreality is gradually removed over time to reveal a more sympathetic character. The character needs to be dragged toward the reader in form or philosophy.

10. It isn't made clear which editor's course is discussed; the editors' introduction doesn't distinguish between writers' voices, resulting in an interesting simultaneity of voice if not mode.

11. My students tell me that children relate to animals (apparently more than with child characters); if there is identification here it likely has more to do with other things. That White makes the spider the title character suggests with whom his interests lay, and his obvious research on spiders notwithstanding, it isn't likely with spiderness.

12. I am certain that Sister Patricia omitted this information when she read it aloud to my fifth-grade class.

13. Ironically, Frye lists animals, women, and children as potentially more pathetic as character choices. Most notable as it relates to the animal fantasy *Charlotte's Web*, Frye couples the statement that "the central figure of pathos is often a woman or a child" with his observation that "the death of an animal is usually pathetic" (38–39). That Charlotte should achieve the status of high mimetic is remarkable, apparently!

14. Nikolajeva goes on to say that "if we only read the novel on the mimetic level, it is a tragedy. Leslie is dead. . . . However, Katherine Paterson has herself rejected this view of her work. On the symbolic level, Leslie has played out her

role, and it does not really matter anymore" (*Rhetoric* 110). I would argue that while we might understand Leslie's death on the symbolic level as well as on the mimetic level, the former doesn't or shouldn't trump the latter. We benefit by acknowledging both understandings; we are then able to consider the relative use of each of those ways of processing the text.

15. Death can be spun, and it can be spun by mode. Leslie's death can be limited to irony, or it can be the catalyst to another's growth. Charlotte's death could have been reconsidered as a wasted isolation in her last hours should Wilbur fail to safeguard her eggs or be turned to bacon on his return. History and the news media have always used mode to tell the stories of death; any person's death might be cast in any of the four modes with surprising ease. Children's literature's many representations of death might be thought of as expressions of mode. The characters of these books with entwining modes influence—determine—each others' stories and meanings through their actions. It requires two persons' stories, perhaps, so that mutual illumination can result. Anyone who has read Chris Raschka's *Arlene Sardine* knows how death can be made absurd through the incongruity of romance and irony in one character's story. Arlene wants to be a sardine. That's just a bad dream for a fish (or anyone else, I suppose). If Arlene's is the story of fulfilling one's dream, it's made ridiculous by the dream being a death wish. I read that book aloud to my students every term; they are either horrified or delighted. Those who are horrified are thinking about the children and their protection; those who are delighted are responding to the story as it must be—as absurdity, an absurdity born of turning romance into irony. The disconnect is purposeful, as is the move to entwine contrasting modes through two different characters.

16. Peter Neumeyer observes that "in *Charlotte's Web*, the incidents follow inevitably, fate seems inexorable, and, in fact, we have no cheap romance, but tragicomedy in which salvation comes hand in hand with the cathartic ending in which Charlotte is sacrificed for the continuity of her species" (74). I agree with the reading of mode, but I don't think Charlotte's ending is inevitable for the reader of any age.

17. Characters who have evoked in my students' confusion about how to feel also include Gordy from Sherman Alexie's *The Absolutely True Diary of a Part-Time Indian*, Charlie in Steven Chbosky's *The Perks of Being a Wallflower*, and Min Green in Daniel Handler's *Why We Broke Up*. In all of these cases, the authors communicate humor and sympathy in a way that keeps us from investing in either direction.

18. A possible exception comes in the form of the mother in Robert Munsch's *Love You Forever*. Over the course of the picture book, the mother is modulated visually from representational woman to a caricature of a Victorian miniature of an old woman—small, round, gray-bunned, and dressed in generic "old woman clothes"—and is even set in what looks to be a less modern room than the ones she inhabits as young mother. Even her glasses regress historically. She loses her individuality and becomes simply a generic "old woman." This modulation seems

twinned with the modulation of her son from generic toddler-to-teen to a more nuanced adult male, so it is a balance rather than the focus of the regression of a single protagonist. All of this is visually achieved through illustrations.

Chapter 4

1. How many of us who grew up in front of the television knew in our hearts that an anvil's purpose was to crush bad guys? That this object was chosen for this purpose in cartoons remains to me a constant wonder.

2. Falling from a height into the abyss seems a favorite Disney disposal method for baddies: Gaston, the Evil Queen in *Snow White*, Maleficent in *Sleeping Beauty*, Cruella in *101 Dalmatians*, Frollo in *The Hunchback of Notre Dame*, Clayton in *Tarzan*, and Ratigan in *The Great Mouse Detective*. It is a clean death off camera, and unlike, say, a wolf being chased off into the woods, the implication is that the fall is not survived.

3. The protagonist, a young boy, is never named in Dahl's book.

4. Michael Levy and Farah Mendlesohn describe James's aunts as "grotesques" and note that Dahl's adult, female characters are usually either "saints or sinners" (109–10).

Bibliography

Primary Sources

Alcott, Louisa May. *Little Women*. Roberts Brothers, 1868.
Alexander, Lloyd. *The High King*. Dell, 1968.
Anderson, M. T. *Feed*. Candlewick, 2002.
Babbitt, Natalie. *Tuck Everlasting*. Farrar, Straus and Giroux, 1988.
Banks, Lynne Reid. *The Indian in the Cupboard*. Doubleday, 1980.
Barnhill, Kelly. *The Girl Who Drank the Moon*. Algonquin Young Readers, 2016.
Barrie, James. *Peter Pan in Kensington Garden*. Arthur Rackham, 1906.
Baum, L. Frank. *The Wonderful Wizard of Oz*. Dover, 1960.
Bell, Cece. *El Deafo*. Harry N. Abrams, 2014
Block, Francesca Lia. *Weetzie Bat*. HarperTrophy, 1989.
Brink, Carol Ryrie. *Caddie Woodlawn*. Macmillan, 1935.
Brown, Marc. *Arthur's Nose*. Little, Brown and Company, 1976.
Brown, Marc. *Arthur Turns Green*. Little, Brown and Company, 2011.
Bryant, Jen. *Pieces of Georgia*. Yearling, 2006.
Bunting, Eve. *Fly Away Home*. Scholastic, 1991.
Bunting, Eve. *Smoky Night*. Harcourt, 1994.
Bunting, Eve. *The Wall*. Scholastic, 1990.
Burnett, Frances Hodgson. *The Secret Garden*. Laurel Leaf Books, 1987.
Chbosky, Stephen. *The Perks of Being a Wallflower*. MTV Books, 1999.
Collins, Suzanne. *The Hunger Games*. Scholastic, 2008.
Collins, Suzanne. *Mockingjay*. Scholastic, 2010.
Cooper, Susan. *The Dark Is Rising*. Random House, 1973.
Coraline. Dir. Henry Selick. Laika, 2009. Film.
Cormier, Robert. *The Chocolate War*. Pantheon Books, 1974.
Dahl, Roald. *James and the Giant Peach*. Scholastic, 1988.
Dahl, Roald. *Matilda*. Puffing Books, 1988.
Dahl, Roald. *Witches*. Puffing Books, 1983.

DiCamillo, Kate. *The Tale of Despereaux*. Candlewick, 2003.
DuPrau, Jeanne. *The City of Ember*. Yearling, 2003.
Funke, Cornelia. *Inkheart*. Scholastic, 2011.
Gaiman, Neil. *Coraline*. HarperCollins, 2002.
Gaiman, Neil. *Coraline*. Adapted and illustrated by P. Craig Russell. HarperCollins, 2008.
Gantos, Jack. *Joey Pigza Swallowed the Key*. Farrar, Straus and Giroux, 1998.
Hesse, Karen. *Witness*. Scholastic, 2003.
Hinton, S. E. *The Outsiders*. Viking, 1967.
Hopkins, Ellen. *Crank*. Simon and Schuster, 2004.
How the Grinch Stole Christmas. Dir. Ron Howard. Universal, 2000. Film.
Jones, Diana Wynne. *Howl's Moving Castle*. Greenwillow Books, 1986.
Le Guin, Ursula K. *Tehanu*. Atheneum, 1990.
Le Guin, Ursula K. *A Wizard of Earthsea*. Bantam, 1975 [orig. publ. 1968].
Levine, Gail Carson. *Ella Enchanted*. HarperTeen, 2004.
Lewis, C. S. *The Last Battle*. Harper Trophy, 1970.
Lewis, C. S. *The Lion, the Witch, and the Wardrobe*. Harper Trophy, 1970.
Lofting, Hugh. *The Story of Doctor Dolittle*. Frederick A. Stokes, 1920.
Lowry, Lois. *The Giver*. Houghton Mifflin, 1993.
Lowry, Lois. *Number the Stars*. Houghton Mifflin Harcourt, 1989.
McGraw, Eloise. *The Moorchild*. New York: Aladdin, 2006.
McKinley, Robin. *Beauty*. HarperTrophy, 1978.
McKinley, Robin. *The Blue Sword*. Greenwillow, 1982.
Medina, Meg. *Burn Baby Burn*. Candlewick, 2013.
Meyer, Marissa. *Cinder*. Feiwel and Friends, 2012.
Meyer, Stephenie. *Twilight*. Little, Brown and Company, 2005.
Munsch, Robert. *Love You Forever*. Firefly Books, 1986.
Norton, Mary. *The Borrowers*. J. M. Dent, 1952.
Okorafor, Nnedi. *Akata Witch*. Viking, 2011.
Paterson, Katherine. *Bridge to Terabithia*. Avon Books, 1977.
Paulsen, Gary. *Woodsong*. Simon and Schuster, 2007.
Pratchett, Terry. *A Hat Full of Sky*. HarperCollins, 2004.
Pullman, Philip. *His Dark Materials*. Scholastic, 1995–2000.
Raschka, Chris. *Arlene Sardine*. Orchard Books, 1998.
Rowling, J. K. *Harry Potter and the Deathly Hallows*. Scholastic, 2009.
Rowling, J. K. *Harry Potter and the Half-Blood Prince*. Scholastic, 2005.
Rowling, J. K. *Harry Potter and the Prisoner of Azkaban*. Scholastic, 1999.
Rowling, J. K. *Harry Potter and the Sorcerer's Stone*. Scholastic, 1997.
Santa Claus Is Coming to Town. Dir. Arthur Rankin Jr. and Jules Bass. Rankin/Bass Productions, 1970. Film.
Schanzer, Robin. *Witches!* National Geographic Children's Books, 2011.
Sendak, Maurice. *Where the Wild Things Are*. HarperCollins, 1984.

Steig, William. *Shrek*. Farrar, Straus and Giroux, 1990.
Stone, Jon. *The Monster at the End of This Book*. Golden Books, 1994.
Tan, Shaun. *The Arrival*. Hodder and Stroughton, 2006.
Waber, Bernard. *Ira Says Goodbye*. Houghton Mifflin, 1988.
Waber, Bernard. *Ira Sleeps Over*. Houghton Mifflin, 1972.
Who Framed Roger Rabbit? Dir. Robert Zemeckis. Walt Disney Animation Studios, 1988. Film.
White, E. B. *Charlotte's Web*. HarperCollins, 2001.
Wiesner, David. *Tuesday*. Houghton Mifflin Harcourt, 1991.
Willhoite, Michael. *Daddy's Roommate*. Alyson Books, 1990.
Williams-Garcia, Rita. *One Crazy Summer*. Amistad, 2010.
Woodson, Jacqueline. *The Other Side*. G. P. Putnam's Sons, 2001.
Yang, Gene Luen. *American Born Chinese*. First Second, 2006.

Secondary Sources

"Back Dorm Boys. I Want It That Way." http://www.youtube.com/watch?v=YBlC tqsat-w.
Bal, Mieke. *Narratology: Introduction to the Theory of Narrative*. 2nd ed. U of Toronto P, 1997 [1985].
Barker, Jani. "Virtuous Transgressors, Not Moral Saints: Protagonists in Contemporary Children's Literature." In *Ethics and Children's Literature*, edited by Claudia Mills, Routledge, 2014, pp. 101–24.
Bawden, Nina. "A Dead Pig and My Father." *Children's Literature in Education*, vol. 5, no. 2, 1974, pp. 3–13.
Bayliss, Sarah. "How 'El Deafo' Empowers Kids Who Are Deaf and Hard of Hearing." *School Library Journal* January 30, 2017 http://www.slj.com/2017/01/diversity/how-el-deafo-empowers-kids-who-are-deaf-and-hearing-impaired/#_.
Bernaerts, Lars, Marco Caracciolo, Luc Herman, and Bart Vervaeck. "The Storied Lives of Non-Human Narrators." *Narrative*, vol. 22, no. 1, January 2014, pp. 68–93.
Booth, Wayne C. *The Company We Keep: An Ethics of Fiction*. U of California P, 1988.
Booth, Wayne C. *A Rhetoric of Fiction*. U of Chicago P, 1961.
Booth, Wayne C. *A Rhetoric of Irony*. U of Chicago P, 1974.
Cadden, Mike. "All Is Well: The Epilogue in Children's Fantasy Fiction." *Narrative*, vol. 20, no. 3, Fall 2012, pp. 343–56.
Cadden, Mike. "Home Is a Matter of Blood, Time, and Genre: Essentialism in Burnett and McKinley." *ARIEL: A Review of International English Literature*, vol. 28, no. 1, 1997, pp. 53–67.

Cadden, Mike. "The Irony of Narration in the Young Adult Novel." *Children's Literature Association Quarterly*, vol. 25, no. 3, pp. 146–54.

Cadden, Mike. "Purposeful Movement among People and Places: The Sense of Home in Ursula K. Le Guin's Fiction for Children and Adults." *Extrapolation*, vol. 41, no. 4, Winter 2000, pp. 338–50

Cadden, Mike. "Simultaneous Emotions: Entwining Modes in Children's Books." *Children's Literature in Education: An International Quarterly*, vol. 36, no. 3, September, 2005, pp. 285–98.

Cadden, Mike. "Speaking to the Needs of Genre: Le Guin's Ethics of Audience." *The Lion and the Unicorn: A Critical Journal of Children's Literature*, vol. 24, no. 1, 2000, pp. 128–42.

Chambers, Aidan. "The Reader in the Book." In *Children's Literature: The Development of Criticism*. ed., Peter Hunt, Routledge, 1990, pp. 91–114.

Chaston, Joel. "The Other Deaths in Bridge to Terabithia." *Children's Literature Association Quarterly*, vol. 16, no. 4, Winter 1991–92, pp. 238–41.

Chatman, Seymour. "The 'Rhetoric' 'of' 'Fiction.'" *Reading Narrative: Form, Ethics, Ideology*. ed., James Phelan. Ohio State UP, 1989, pp. 40–56.

Clausen, Christopher. "Home and Away in Children's Fiction." *Children's Literature*, vol. 10, 1982, pp. 141–52.

Coats, Karen. *The Bloomsbury Introduction to Children's and Young Adult Literature*. Bloomsbury, 2018.

Coats, Karen. "Fish Stories: Teaching Children's Literature in a Postmodern World." *Pedagogy: Critical Approaches to Teaching Literature, Language, Composition, and Culture*, vol. 1, no. 2, Spring 2001, pp. 405–09.

Coats, Karen. "Keepin' It Plural: Children's Studies in the Academy." *Children's Literature Association Quarterly*, vol. 26, no. 3, Fall 2001, pp. 140–50.

Colbert, Stephen. "Grim Colberty Talks with Maurice Sendak." *The Colbert Report*. Comedy Central, 24 Jan. 2012. Web. 4 Dec. 2016.

Collinson, Roger. "The Children's Author and His Readers." *Children's Literature in Education: An International Quarterly*, vol. 10, 1973, pp. 37–49.

Crawford, Philip Charles. "Review of *American Born Chinese* by Gene Luen Yang." *School Library Journal*, vol. 52, no. 9, Sept. 2006, pp. 240.

"Curious George." *Curious about George?* Houghton Mifflin Harcourt Publishing Company, n.d. Web. 04 Dec. 2016.

Dickson, Randi. "Horror: To Gratify, Not Edify." *Language Arts*, vol. 76, no. 2, 1998, pp. 115–22.

Dong, Lan. "Reimagining the Monkey King in Comics: Gene Luen Yang's *American Born Chinese*." In *Oxford Handbook of Children's Literature*, edited by Julia Mickenberg and Lynne Vallone, Oxford UP, pp. 231–51.

Doughty, Jonathan. "More than Meets the 'I': Chinese Transnationality in Gene Luen Yang's *American Born Chinese*." *Asian American Literature: Discourses and Pedagogies*, no. 1, 2010, pp. 54–60.

Finn, Joyce. "For Beginners Only." *Writers' Journal*, vol. 30, no. 5, Sept./Oct. 2009, pp. 57–58.

Flynn, Richard. "The Intersection of Children's Literature and Childhood Studies." *Children's Literature Association Quarterly*, vol. 22, no. 3, Fall 1997, pp. 143–45.

Forster, E. M. *Aspects of the Novel.* Harcourt Brace, 1985 [1927].

Fraustino, Lisa. "The Rights and Wrongs of Anthropomorphism in Picture Books." In *Ethics and Children's Literature*, edited by Claudia Mills. Ashgate, 2014, pp. 145–62.

Frye, Northrop. *Anatomy of Criticism: Four Essays.* Princeton UP, 1957.

Galbraith, Mary. "Hear My Cry: A Manifesto for an Emancipatory Childhood Studies Approach to Children's Literature." *The Lion and the Unicorn*, vol. 25, no. 2, April 2001, pp. 187–205.

Gardner, Jared. "Same Difference: Graphic Alterity in the Work of Gene Luen Yang, Adrian Tomine, and Derek Kirk Kim." In *Multicultural Comics: From Zap to Blue Beetle*, edited by Frederick Luis Aldama. U of Texas P, 2010, pp. 132–47.

Griffith, John. "*Charlotte's Web*: A Lonely Fantasy of Love." *Children's Literature*, vol. 8, 1979, pp. 111–17.

Gubar, Marah. "On Not Defining Children's Literature." *PMLA*, vol. 126, no. 1, January 2011, pp. 209–16.

Gubar, Marah. "Species Trouble: The Abjection of Adolescence in E. B. White's *Stuart Little*." *The Lion and the Unicorn*, vol. 27, no. 1, January 2003, pp. 98–119.

Haddon, Mark. "Mark Haddon on His Best Seller, *The Curious Incident of the Dog in the Night-Time*." *The Observer*. Guardian News and Media, 11 Apr. 2004. Web. Dec. 2016.

Hathaway, Rosemary V. "'More than Meets the Eye': Transformative Intertextuality in Gene Luen Yang's *American Born Chinese*." *The ALAN Review*, vol. 37, no. 1, Fall 2009, pp. 41–47.

Henderson, Eleanor. "I Wasn't Born Yesterday: The Beauty of Backstory." *Poets & Writers*, vol. 41, no. 5, Sept./Oct. 2013, pp. 23–27.

Hentea, Marius. "The Forms and Functions of Back Story in the Novel." *Narrative*, vol. 18, no. 3, Oct. 2010, pp. 347–66.

Hinderer, Moira. "Talking to Children about Race: Children's Literature in a Segregated Era, 1930–1945." In *Ethics and Children's Literature*, edited by Claudia Mills. Ashgate, 2014, pp. 41–55.

Hixon, Martha. "'Whose Woods These Are I Think I Know': Narrative Theory and Diana Wynne Jones's *Hexwood*." In *Telling Children's Stories: Narrative Theory and Children's Literature*, edited by Mike Cadden, U of Nebraska P, 2010, pp. 251–67.

Hunter, Mollie. *Talent Is Not Enough.* Harper & Row, 1976.

Keen, Suzanne. *Empathy and the Novel.* Oxford UP, 2010.

Kermode, Frank. *The Sense of an Ending: Studies in the Theory of Fiction*. Oxford UP, 1966.

Kertzer, Adrienne. "Cinderella's Stepsisters, Traumatic Memory, and Young People's Writing." *The Lion and the Unicorn*, vol. 40, no. 1, 2016, pp. 1–21.

Kinghorn, Norton D. "The Real Miracle of *Charlotte's Web*." *Children's Literature Association Quarterly*, vol. 11, no. 1, Spring 1986, pp. 4–9.

Knoepflmacher, U. C., and Mitzi Myers. "From the Editors: 'Cross-Writing' and the Reconceptualization of Children's Literary Studies." *Children's Literature*, vol. 25, 1997, pp. vii–xvii.

Le Guin, Ursula K. *Dancing at the Edge of the World: Thoughts on Words, Women, Places*. Harper & Row, 1989, pp. 37–45.

Le Guin, Ursula K. *Earthsea Revisioned*. Green Bay, 1993.

Le Guin, Ursula K. "Introduction." *A Fisherman of the Inland Sea: Science Fiction Stories*. HarperPrism, 1994, pp. 1–11.

Le Guin, Ursula K. "A Response, by Ansible, from Tau Ceti." *Words Are My Matter: Writings about Life and Books 2000–2016*. Small Beer 2017.

Le Guin, Ursula K. "Why Are Americans Afraid of Dragons?" *The Language of the Night: Essays on Fantasy and Science Fiction*. HarperPerennial, 1989, pp. 34–40.

L'Engle, Madeleine. *A Circle of Quiet*. HarperOne, 1984.

L'Engle, Madeleine. "Genesis Trilogy." *Madeleine L'Engle*. Crosswicks, 29 Aug. 2011. Web. 04 Dec. 2016.

Levy, Michael, and Farah Mendlesohn. *Children's Fantasy Literature: An Introduction*. Cambridge UP, 2016.

Lewis, C. S. "On Three Ways of Writing for Children." *The Riverside Anthology of Children's Literature*, edited by Judith Saltman 6th ed. Houghton Mifflin, 1985, pp. 1075–81.

Lukens, Rebecca. *A Critical Handbook of Children's Literature*. Pearson, 1976.

McCallum, Robyn. *Ideologies of Identity in Adolescent Fiction*. Garland, 1999.

McCort, Jessica R. *Reading in the Dark: Horror in Children's Literature and Culture*. UP of Mississippi, 2016.

Mills, Claudia. Introduction. *Ethics and Children's Literature*, edited by Claudia Mills, Ashgate, 2014, pp. 1–12.

Morgenstern, John. "Children and Other Talking Animals." *The Lion and the Unicorn*, vol. 24, no. 1, January 2000, pp. 110–27.

Muecke, D. C. *The Compass of Irony*. Methuen, 1969.

Neumeyer, Peter. "What Makes a Good Children's Book? The Texture of *Charlotte's* Web." *Critical Essays on E. B. White*, edited by Robert L. Root, Jr., G. K. Hall, 1994, pp. 69–77.

Nikolajeva, Maria. *Aesthetics of Children's Literature*. Scarecrow, 2005.

Nikolajeva, Maria. *Children's Literature Comes of Age: Toward a New Aesthetic*. Garland, 1996.

Nikolajeva, Maria. "The Identification Fallacy." *Telling Children's Stories*, edited by Mike Cadden, U of Nebraska P, 2011, pp. 187–208.

Nikolajeva, Maria. *Reading for Learning: Cognitive Approaches to Children's Literature.* John Benjamins, 2014.
Nikolajeva, Maria. *The Rhetoric of Character in Children's Literature.* Scarecrow, 2002.
Nodelman, Perry. *The Hidden Adult.* Johns Hopkins UP, 2009.
Nodelman, Perry. *Words about Pictures: The Narrative Art of Children's Picture Books.* U of Georgia P, 1988.
Nodelman, Perry, and Mavis Reimer. *The Pleasures of Children's Literature.* 3rd ed. Pearson, 2002.
Nussbaum, Martha. *Love's Knowledge: Essays on Philosophy and Literature.* Oxford UP, 1992.
Painter, Clare, J. R. Martin, and Len Unsworth. *Reading Visual Narratives: Image Analysis of Children's Picture Books.* Equinox, 2013.
Paterson, Katherine. *Gates of Excellence: On Reading and Writing Books for Children.* Elsevier/Nelson Books, 1981.
Phelan, James. *Experiencing Fiction: Judgments, Progressions, and the Rhetorical Theory of Narrative.* Ohio State UP, 2007.
Phelan, James. *Narrative as Rhetoric: Technique, Audiences, Ethics, Ideology.* Ohio State UP, 1996.
Phelan, James. *Reading People, Reading Plots: Character, Progression, and the Interpretation of Narrative.* U of Chicago P, 1989.
Phelan, James, and Peter J. Rabinowitz. "Narrative as Rhetoric." In *Narrative Theory: Core Concepts and Critical Debates*, edited by David Herman, James Phelan, Peter J. Rabinowitz, Brian Richardson, and Robyn Warhol, Ohio State UP, 2012, pp. 3–8.
Pratchett, Terry. "Talking with Terry Pratchett." In *A Hat Full of Sky*, HarperCollins, 2004.
Pullman, Philip. "Intention." In *Keywords for Children's Literature*, edited by Philip Nel and Lissa Paul, New York UP, 2011.
Rabinowitz, Peter J. *Before Reading: Narrative Convention and the Politics of Interpretation.* Ohio State UP, 1987.
Rose, Jacqueline. *The Case of Peter Pan, or the Impossibility of Children's Fiction.* U of Pennsylvania P, 1992.
Ross, Ashley. "J. K. Rowling Reveals New Harry Potter Backstory on Pottermore." *Time.Com*, 24 June 2015. EBSCOhost.
Sainsbury, Lisa. *Ethics in British Children's Literature: Unexamined Life.* Bloomsbury, 2015.
Saldívar, Ramón. "The Second Elevation of the Novel: Race, Form, and the Postrace Aesthetic in Contemporary Narrative." *Narrative*, vol. 21, no. 1, January 2013, pp. 1–18.
Scholes, Robert, and Robert Kellogg. *The Nature of Narrative.* Oxford UP, 1968.
Segel, Elizabeth. "Realism and Children's Literature: Notes from a Historical Perspective." *Children's Literature Association Quarterly*, vol. 5, no. 3, Fall 1980, pp. 15–18.

Sloan, Glenna Davis. *The Child as Critic*. Teacher's College, 1975.

Song, Min Hyoung. "'How Good It Is to Be a Monkey': Comics, Racial Formation, and *American Born Chinese*." *Mosaic*, vol. 43, no. 1, March 2010, pp. 73–93.

Stewart, Mark. "Beverly Cleary: Kids like Us." *Columns Magazine*. University of Washington, Sept. 2008. Web. 04 Dec. 2016.

Stott, Jon C. "Running Away to Home—A Story Pattern in Children's Literature." *Language Arts*, vol. 55, no. 4, 1978, pp. 473–77.

Stott, Jon C., and Christine Doyle Francis. "'Home' and 'Not Home' in Children's Stories: Getting There—and Being Worth It." *Children's Literature in Education: An International Quarterly*, vol. 24, no. 3, 1993, pp. 223–33.

Tarr, Anita. "The Absence of Moral Agency in Robert Cormier's *The Chocolate War*." *Children's Literature*, vol. 30, 2002, pp. 96–124.

Trites, Roberta Seelinger. *Disturbing the Universe: Power and Repression in Adolescent Literature*. U of Iowa P, 2000.

Trites, Roberta Seelinger. *Literary Conceptualizations of Growth: Metaphors and Cognition in Adolescent Literature*. John Benjamins, 2014.

Tunnell, Michael O., and James S. Jacobs. *Children's Literature, Briefly*. 2nd ed. Prentice Hall, 1999.

Wall, Barbara. *The Narrator's Voice: The Dilemma of Children's Fiction*. St. Martin's, 1991.

Walsh, Jill Patton. "The Writers in the Writer: A Reply to Hugh Crago." *Signal*, vol. 40, 1983, pp. 3–11.

Walsh, Jill Patton. "The Writer's Responsibility." *Children's Literature in Education: An International Quarterly*, vol. 10, 1973, pp. 30–36.

Walsh, Richard. *The Rhetoric of Fictionality: Narrative Theory and the Idea of Fiction*. Ohio State UP, 2007.

Wimsatt, M. K., and M. C. Beardsley. "The Intentional Fallacy." In *Critical Theory Since Plato*, edited by Hazard Adams, Harcourt Brace Jovanovich, 1971, pp. 1015–22.

Wyile, Andrea Schwenke. "First-Person Engaging Narration in the Picture Book: Verbal and Pictorial Variations." *Children's Literature in Education*, vol. 32, no. 3, 2001, pp. 191–202.

Yang, Gene Luen. "Printz Award Winner Speech." *Young Adult Library Services*, vol. 6, no. 1, 2007, pp. 11–13.

Index

About the Author

Photo credit Melissa Cox

Mike Cadden is past president of the Children's Literature Association. He is author of *Ursula K. Le Guin beyond Genre: Fiction for Children and Adults* and editor of *Telling Children's Stories: Narrative Theory and Children's Literature* and *Teaching Young Adult Literature*.

Printed in Poland
by Amazon Fulfillment
Poland Sp. z o.o., Wrocław

12368075R00094